A GROUNDED FAITH:

Reconnecting with Creator and Creation in the Season of Lent

A Lenten Companion to
Becoming Rooted: One Hundred Days of Reconnecting with Sacred Earth
by Dr. Randy Woodley (Broadleaf, 2022)

Rev. Dr. Janet L. Parker and Rev. Solveig Nilsen-Goodin, eds.

A Grounded Faith

Reconnecting with Creator and Creation
in the Season of Lent

Barclay Press, Inc.
Newberg, Oregon
www.barclaypress.com

Interior illustrations by James Kegley

Cover art by Yongha Bae

Unless otherwise noted, Scripture quotations are from
The Inclusive Bible: The First Egalitarian Translation,
copyright © 2007 Priests for Equality, Rowman & Littlefield Publishers, Inc.
All rights reserved.

Printed in the United States of America.

ISBN 978-1-59498-083-1

ACKNOWLEDGMENTS

The vision for this book began as a question: How might we invite and encourage people of Christian faith to engage Dr. Randy Woodley's important new book, *Becoming Rooted: One Hundred Days of Reconnecting with Sacred Earth?* What resulted is far beyond anything we had imagined with that initial question. And it would never have taken shape without the collaboration of a remarkable number of people who threw their hearts into this project.

First and foremost, the editors want to thank Dr. Randy Woodley for blessing and assisting in the creation of this resource. He immediately understood the value of having a devotional that was specifically written for Christian congregations and individuals who would be reading his book during the season of Lent. We created this book entirely for the purpose of helping churches engage with Dr. Woodley's message and connect it to their own faith commitments. We also wanted to elevate the profile of Randy and Edith Woodley's amazing work as co-sustainers of Eloheh Indigenous Center for Earth Justice and Eloheh Farm and Seeds—a beacon of hope for those of us who live in their watershed and beyond.

We could not have produced this book without permission and assistance from Broadleaf Books, the publisher of *Becoming Rooted.* We are so grateful that Broadleaf granted permission for us to bring Dr. Woodley's voice directly into this devotional through the quotes that are featured at the beginning of each day's reflection. We also thank Broadleaf for the permission to use artist James Kegley's beautiful branch image at the beginning of each daily devotion, thus providing a visual link between *A Grounded Faith* and *Becoming Rooted.* We deeply appreciate Valerie Weaver-Zercher from Broadleaf, who went above and beyond in helping us secure these permissions.

We knew that it would be challenging to bring this publication to print in time for Lent in 2022. Our first plan, in fact, was for a simple booklet created "in-house" by staff from EcoFaith Recovery. Then Cherice Bock, one of our writers, stepped up and connected us with our publisher, Barclay

Press, and Barclay's publisher and CEO, Eric Muhr. We could not have asked for a better partner to bring *A Grounded Faith* into publication. Eric has believed in this project from the outset and assisted us every step of the way. We also wish to thank the other staff at Barclay who worked on this project and brought it to fruition.

This book was born from partnerships between EcoFaith Recovery (ecofaithrecovery.org), Eloheh Indigenous Center for Earth Justice (eloheh.org), and Ecumenical Ministries of Oregon (emoregon.org). It would not have been possible if individuals from these organizations had not already developed relationships of trust with one another, and we are deeply grateful that this project provided an opportunity to further strengthen these relationships and partnerships.

Finally, the concept for this book would have remained a mere dream without the incredible team of writers who agreed, at short notice, to make this dream a reality. The editors wish to thank all of the writers (see About the Authors) who each brought their unique voice and perspective to this project. The editors have been enlightened, moved, and challenged by the way each writer has engaged Scripture, Dr. Woodley's book, Lenten themes and their own life histories in creating their reflections. We truly believe that this is a Lenten devotional like no other, and we are grateful to our Creator for giving us the opportunity to bring this gift into the world.

TABLE OF CONTENTS

FOREWORD

I am honored to have my book, *Becoming Rooted: One Hundred Days of Reconnecting with Sacred Earth*, be used to inspire this Lenten devotional. I share this for several reasons. First of all, because the authors in this book are all friends of mine, and few things feel better to a person than having friends who believe in you and the work you are doing. For this, I am deeply grateful and touched to the heart. Secondly, I am a Follower of Jesus. Anything that we can do to honor Creator-Son and his journey from time immemorial to time everlasting, especially concerning his life, is worthwhile. The more I study the life of Jesus, especially through Indigenous eyes, the smaller I feel while taking a long view of history and future, and the larger I feel knowing I am loved by the Creator.

The greatest sense of the honor that I feel because of this book, though, has to do with my third and final reason. The Western, modern, colonized, industrial world is missing something important. This gap, obvious to Indigenous peoples, also exists among the people of faith who have been affected by the Western worldview. In one sense, we have all been traumatized by the projects of Empire. We are all, by some measure, victims of our times. We are also perpetrators of colonial patterns and Western thinking that have harmed people and the community of creation around us, which also includes people. There are tremendous parallels between how Empire has treated people groups and how it has treated the rest of the community of creation or the Earth. The bottom line is this: we must take responsibility for the world we are a part of and to which we contribute, whether our influence be good or bad. If there is any way for me to bridge this gap between a worldview that destroys and a worldview that builds up, I want to be there.

The Western worldview will not sustain us into the future; our time is running out. It is a time when all people, including people of faith, come to realize that there is a deep need to understand our Creator through creation. To Indigenous peoples, this is natural. To the modern, Western thinker, a wall exists to keep humans believing they are separate from and above nature. I desire to give everyone the "go-ahead" to do what they naturally want to do but, unnaturally, have been taught not to do; that is, to once again fall in love with creation, in the same way Jesus loves creation. As a result, you will learn more about Creator-Jesus.

So please, enjoy the Scriptures, quotes from my book and reflections of my friends who are also on this journey with me. I am glad that you have joined the journey into Jesus' connection with creation. By it, I think you will discover or re-discover your own connections!

—Dr. Randy Woodley

INTRODUCTION

Context

I have never been as ready for the season of Lent as I am this year. It's admittedly odd to look forward to Lent. It is such a somber season, with its exhortations to "remember that we are dust," to "take up our cross and follow Jesus," to "repent for our sins," and to "give up something for Lent." My longing for Lent this year stems from the dis-ease that I am feeling about the state of our world.

We are living through a pivotal moment in the history of humanity. We are facing a series of tests created not by our loving God but by the fateful choices of past and present generations of humans. Will life as human beings have known it for the past 11,000 years continue? Our generation will decide. We didn't choose this responsibility, but it is ours nonetheless.

So I am ready for Lent because Lent is that season of the Christian year that calls us to serious reflection and to the practice of repentance—of "turning around" and "changing our minds." We repent from destructive addictions and behaviors and submit ourselves to the dying and rising process that Jesus initiated so that we can come into the new life that Christ promised. But Christians can no longer pretend that we can do this work alone, particularly not those who have predominantly Anglo-European heritage. Christians need help, especially from traditions who know how to live in harmony with Earth—the only viable home we have. We need to listen to Indigenous voices, both within and outside the Christian tradition, who are calling us back to our original God-given vocation to be Earthkeepers (Gen. 1:26–2:15).

Invitation

Along with the other writers of *A Grounded Faith: Reconnecting with Creator and Creation in the Season of Lent,* I am thrilled to invite you into a journey inspired by the wisdom of Dr. Randy Woodley and his new book, *Becoming Rooted: One Hundred Days of Reconnecting with Sacred Earth*. This devotional, *A Grounded Faith*, is intended to be a Lenten companion to *Becoming Rooted*, although it can also be used as a standalone Lenten resource.

Dr. Woodley is a Cherokee descendant recognized by the United Keetoowah Band and is one of those rare individuals who balances activism and academia, working with words and working with the land. He is the Distinguished Professor of Faith and Culture at Portland Seminary in Oregon and the author of many books. With his wife Edith, an Eastern Shoshone tribal member, he is creating and co-sustaining the Eloheh Indigenous Center for Earth Justice, and Eloheh Farm and Seeds, on a beautiful plot of God's creation in Yamhill, Oregon. With Dr. Woodley and *Becoming Rooted* as our guide, the writers of this devotional invite you to reconnect with Creator and creation this Lent, not only for your personal benefit but for the life of the world.

The idea for this devotional arose out of a budding partnership between the interfaith leadership development network, EcoFaith Recovery, and Eloheh Indigenous Center for Earth Justice in the fall of 2021. Dr. Woodley invited EcoFaith Recovery and another of EcoFaith's partner organizations, Ecumenical Ministries of Oregon, to help bring *Becoming Rooted* to our networks. We eagerly accepted this invitation, and leaders in EcoFaith Recovery and Ecumenical Ministries of Oregon are among the writers of this devotional. Other writers of this resource are on the Eloheh board. As we pondered how to help Dr. Woodley invite others into the inaugural 100-day journey of reading *Becoming Rooted* in the winter/spring of 2022, we saw the great opportunity that the timing presented: Lent. We realized that a Lenten resource would aid Christian individuals and congregations to connect the vital message of *Becoming Rooted* with Christian faith and Lenten themes.

How It Works

In *A Grounded Faith*, seven writers offer reflections for the seven weeks of Lent (including Holy Week) that engage with Scripture and with the themes of *Becoming Rooted*. Each week in the devotional is tied to one or more of the ten sections of *Becoming Rooted*, which are identified in the Table of Contents. Thus the first week of Lent connects to the first two sections of *Becoming Rooted*, the second week of Lent ties into the next section of *Becoming Rooted*, and so on. Each day's devotion begins with a quote from Scripture and a quote from *Becoming Rooted*, continues with a reflection by the writer, and concludes with an invitation for the reader to engage with the material presented. Ideally, you will also have a copy of *Becoming Rooted* and can begin by reading the chapter in Dr. Woodley's book referenced in each devotion. We encourage you to consider having a journal or sketch pad with you so that you can write down or draw insights, ideas, commitments or goals that arise for you in relation to that day's reflection and invitation.

You will notice that occasionally two different writers will have chosen the same Scripture passage or will be inviting you into a similar practice for engaging the material. We intentionally left these "duplications," recognizing that the different devotional contexts will reveal unique dimensions of both Scripture and practice. We invite you to engage each one as a fresh offering for your reflection. You will also notice a wide variety of invitations for engagement in these devotions. Some may encourage just a few moments of reflection during the day, while others might suggest researching your family history or the Doctrine of Discovery. Engage each as you are able, knowing that "becoming rooted" and cultivating a "grounded faith" are not Lenten projects but lifelong processes.

Themes and Terminology

You have a very rich resource in your hands (or on your device). Seven individuals from different backgrounds, denominations, and life experiences have brought their own wisdom into dialogue with Scripture and a leading Indigenous voice who follows in the way of Jesus. The result is a hearty, nourishing stew that can fortify us in the winter of our world's discontent. *A Grounded Faith* intentionally enters into serious dialogue with themes drawn from Indigenous wisdom and values and is shaped by anti-racist commitments and anti-oppression convictions. As a result, please be prepared. The reflections at times may make you uncomfortable, raise difficult questions for your faith, or challenge your view of American history and even your family heritage. The authors do not seek to cause discomfort for discomfort's sake. Think of these proddings, rather, as spadework for needed transformations in our Christian faith and secular culture so that our present crucifixions may end in Earth-encompassing resurrection for God's suffering creation. We encourage you to find dialogue partners and soul companions to engage with you in this Lenten practice so that you will not wrestle with these challenges alone. The work of re-rooting Christianity in creation-loving soil is not a solo venture.

Two notes on terminology: *Eloheh* and "indigenous."

Eloheh (pronounced "ay-luh-HAY") is a Cherokee word that means "harmony," "wholeness," "peace," "abundance," and other qualities that have their closest equivalent in the biblical term, *shalom*. Dr. Woodley draws on the Cherokee vision and value of *Eloheh* to invite us all to embrace "the harmony way." Recognizing how far out of harmony we have fallen in our relationships with God, one another, and the rest of creation, Dr. Woodley and the writers of this devotional share reflections on ways to re-align our lives and faith with Creator's vision of *Eloheh/shalom*. That re-alignment will require a sometimes painful process of disentangling our Christian faith from imperialistic, patriarchal, and racist dimensions of Western culture. However, in its place, we are invited to rediscover our true humanity and our place in the whole community of creation.

One way to do so is to remember that even those of us, like myself, who come from 100 percent European stock, have indigenous roots in deep time. As Dr. Woodley explains in the introduction to *Becoming Rooted*, we all have indigenous ancestry; some of us are just farther removed in time and place from it than others. Before being colonized and colonizing others, who were we? And who might we be now if, as Dr. Woodley says, "We can all become more lowercase-*i* indigenous on the land"? Taking the lead from his wisdom, we have adopted his practice of using a capital "*I*" when referring to today's Indigenous peoples and nations and a lower-case "*i*" when referring to all people's ancestral indigeneity.

This devotional is an invitation. It is an invitation to reclaim the possibility of becoming more rooted in your place, of remembering your own deep-time indigeneity, and of learning from Indigenous people who live in the land where you now reside. It is an invitation to repent from destructive ways of understanding and practicing our Christian faith and of living as twenty-first-century Americans. It is an invitation to participate in world-healing practices that are faithful to the One who showed us the way out of the tomb and into abundant life. It is a joy to be invited into your Lenten season. Now, let us join Dr. Randy Woodley in walking "the harmony way" and reconnecting with sacred Earth together.

—Rev. Dr. Janet L. Parker

ABOUT THE AUTHORS

Solveig Nilsen-Goodin (Week One) is ordained in the Lutheran Church (ELCA), received her M.Div. from Harvard Divinity School, and currently expresses her vocation as a grief and life Coach and Spiritual Director with the Interfaith Spiritual Center (interfaithspiritualcenter.com) and through the Oregon Synod Reparations Team. In 2009 she helped found EcoFaith Recovery, and from 2006–2017 she founded and pastored the Wilderness Way Community. Solveig sings and leads grief rituals, writes, and dances. With her husband, Peter, she is raising two boys in the traditional homelands of the Cowlitz, Clackamas, and many other Indigenous peoples (Northeast Portland, Oregon).

Janet Parker (Week Two) is a United Church of Christ pastor, Christian ecofeminist ethicist, and nature mystic who dwells in the ancestral land of the Tualatin band of the Kalapuya people (Beaverton, Oregon). She shares her life with her eco-pastor wife, Robyn Hartwig, and their dog, Crystal, and recognizes that a host of ancestors live with and inside her. She received her M.Div. from Princeton Theological Seminary and Ph.D. in Christian Ethics from Union Theological Seminary (New York). In addition to serving the church, she increasingly feels called to cross-cultural partnerships and serves as the Eloheh Engagement Coordinator for EcoFaith Recovery.

Jim Kealoha Sequeira (Week Three) is Native Hawaiian-Chinese and lives in Vancouver, WA, in Chinook people's land with his wife, Glenna. They have two married children and two grandchildren. He is ordained in the Evangelical Covenant Church (ECC), pastors at Cascade View Covenant Church, received an M.A. in Intercultural Studies from NAIITS, and serves on the Eloheh Indigenous Center for Earth Justice board. He is involved in the work of advancing racial righteousness and was part of the leadership in passing the Repudiation of the Doctrine of Discovery in the ECC.

Joshua Grace (Szczesniak) (Week Four) is a Polish/Irish American street artist, an intercultural learner & educator, and a board member of Eloheh. After undergraduate work at Temple University in African American Studies, he graduated with an M.A. in Intercultural Studies from NAIITS, an Indigenous Learning Community. He lives with his family in the traditional lands of the Lenni Lenape in Philadelphia's Kensington neighborhood, where they together enjoy learning and eating from their biodiverse backyard garden.

Tommy Airey (Week Five) is a post-evangelical pastor and writer born and raised in stolen, unceded land that Acjachemen people call Panhe (South Orange County, California) and is being transformed by the thin place the Potawatomie, Ojibwe, Huron and Odawa named Wawiiatanong (Detroit, Michigan). He and his partner Lindsay are committed to the work of soul accompaniment through radical friendship, intentional gathering, and the written word. Tommy is the co-editor of RadicalDiscipleship.net and the author of *Descending Like a Dove: Adventures in Decolonizing Evangelical Christianity* (2018). He is currently working on his second book, *Conspiracy: A Biblical Spirituality for Breaking Rank*.

Cherice Bock (Week Six) teaches in the Creation Care Program at Portland Seminary of George Fox University and leads Oregon Interfaith Power & Light through Ecumenical Ministries of Oregon. She lives in Kalapuya land in Newberg, Oregon. Bock co-edited *Quakers, Creation Care, and Sustainability* (2019, with Stephen Potthoff) and has published many articles and chapters, including "Watershed Discipleship" in *An Ecotopian Lexicon* (2019). With an M.Div. from Princeton Theological Seminary and an MS in environmental studies from Antioch University New England, she speaks, writes, advocates, and engages in activism at the intersection of religion and climate justice. Learn more at http://chericebock.com.

Michael Ellick (Week Seven) is currently the Director of Public Engagement for Ecumenical Ministries of Oregon but has served as a parish minister, a monk, a community organizer, and a public finance analyst. Raised in the old-growth rainforests near the southern tip of the Salish Sea, Michael later received an M.Div. at Union Theological Seminary in New York. He worked in New York City for almost two decades before moving to NE Portland, the ancestral home of the Cowlitz, Clackamas, and many other Indigenous peoples. In recent years he co-founded The Common Table of Oregon and Reckoning with Racism, interfaith organizing projects rooted in truth, repair, and reconciliation.

FIRST WEEK OF LENT: ASH WEDNESDAY

Becoming Rooted, Day 8,
"The Harmony Way"

You are dust, and to dust you will return.

—Genesis 3:19b

The harmony way is a meaningful whole....The wisdom of Indigenous traditions and stories emphasizes the importance of restoring the relationships that exist among Creator, humans, animals, and the Earth—what I call the community of creation.

—Randy Woodley, *Becoming Rooted*, 25–26

Three Ash Wednesdays in a row changed what this first day in the season of Lent means to me. In doing so, they changed me.

In 2014, the Wilderness Way Community invited people into a Lenten practice of praying outside for forty days. That first Ash Wednesday, I invited my family to do the imposition of ashes—outside. As I was making the cross of ashes on my, then, five-year-old's forehead, I said, "Remember that you are dust..." and before I could finish with "...and to dust you shall return," he jumped in with, "No! We aren't dust; we are stardust!" Out of the mouths of babes. Indeed we are, my son, indeed we are.

The next year, I was helping lead an Ash Wednesday service at the Festival of Radical Discipleship in Oak View, California. The ashes were made of sage from the valley, a valley that exploded in flame two years later in the massive Thomas Fire. In that service, I spoke these words, "Today we receive the sign of the cross with ashes made from burned sage from a valley burning in drought. These ashes are a call to repentance. A call to turn around, to turn again to the very ground of our being and ask: God, how do I live here? Right here? Right now? In this watershed? And in this watershed moment? Remind me, O God, that I am not just dust in general (though our transient, mobile, disconnected-from-place culture might have me believe that). No. To the extent that I drink the water from my watershed, eat the food from my watershed, breathe the air of my watershed, will be buried in my watershed, 'I am my watershed, and to my watershed I shall return.' So that is what you will hear today as you receive the sign of the cross in ashes on your foreheads. 'You are your watershed, and to your watershed you shall return.'"

And finally, 2016. Again I wrangled my family for a homemade imposition of ashes ritual outside. But we had no ashes handy. So, instead, standing at the base of our two-hundred-year-old fir tree, acknowledging the sacredness of this ancestral land not our own, we each leaned over, rubbed our fingers in the dirt, and made the sign of the cross on one another's foreheads. "You are Earth, and to Earth you will return."

Dust. Stardust. Watershed. Ancestors. Earth. Us.

Invitation:

Go outside and, with ashes or dirt, make the sign of the cross on your forehead, using the language that helps you feel your connection to place most deeply.

FIRST WEEK OF LENT: THURSDAY

Becoming Rooted, Day 4,
"What the Plant People are Saying"

Immediately the Spirit drove Jesus out into the wilderness, and he remained there for forty days, and was tempted by Satan. He was with the wild beasts, and the angels looked after him.

—Mark 1:12–13

Humanity has yet to realize the fact that nature is wiser and more powerful than we are. Nature will, without a doubt, outlive us. She knows her mind, and she understands what keeps life in balance.

—Randy Woodley, *Becoming Rooted*, 17

Human. Humus. Humility.

This past summer, my oldest son participated in a nine-day wilderness rite of passage for young men. For two of those nights, they fasted, alone. This experience challenges and deeply humbles the boys-becoming-men—physically, mentally, spiritually. But this year, the rite of passage took place during the "heat dome" event that shot temperatures up to nearly 115 degrees Fahrenheit. The boys, the guides, and the families and friends back home all felt in our bones the vulnerability of human beings relative to the forces of nature.

We picked up our son on a beautiful Sunday afternoon. He survived! They survived! Thanks be to God! But exactly one week later, the Grandview Fire ripped through the exact place where we had welcomed the young men back from. Whatever security we had felt having our son home safely was shaken again. We were humbled again. It could have been otherwise.

The Lenten season traditionally begins with a reflection on Jesus' forty-day sojourn through the wilderness. The reflections in modern, Western, White Christianity often focus exclusively on the temptations Jesus encountered. Sometimes we even equate "humility" with simply the emotional consequence of our lack of willpower to keep up an exercise routine or refrain from eating chocolate.

But Indigenous cultures the world over immediately recognize Jesus' journey as something infinitely deeper—a rite of passage—an initiatory experience that places the human in a relationship of complete and utter dependence upon the humus (Earth) and the Creator of both human and humus.

Human, humus, and humility all come from the same root word, meaning Earth or ground. Being humbled and held by the humus and the Creator of humus, we discover what it is to be more deeply human.

Most of us won't have the opportunity to participate in a wilderness rite of passage. But we can learn with humility from Indigenous peoples who recognize the value of such practices. (And we can learn with even deeper humility why many Indigenous peoples are prevented from practicing such traditions in our present context.)

And we can also simply practice being human by spending time outside in humility, in silence, recognizing our vulnerability, our dependence, our connection as humans with humus and the Creator of all that is.

Invitation:

Spend time outside in silence, observing, feeling, sensing, listening, recognizing with humility your vulnerability and your complete and utter dependence on all life and the Giver of life.

FIRST WEEK OF LENT: FRIDAY

Becoming Rooted, Day 7,
"Nature Speaking"

But turn to the animals, and let them teach you; the birds of the air
will tell you the truth. Listen to the plants of the earth, and learn
from them; let the fish of the sea become your teachers. Who among
all these does not know that the hand of YHWH has done this?

—Job 12:7–9

Talk to animals and then be taught by them. Talk to and
listen to birds. Talk to the Earth and other parts of creation
and expect to be taught from them. Listen to fish attest to
the truth. And recognize Creator's hand in all creation.

—Randy Woodley, *Becoming Rooted*, 24

The first time I visited Norway, the land of my ancestors, my most visceral memory came from our time at the goat seter (summer pasture). My eight-year-old girl's heart could hardly contain my love for the goats. My parents had to tear me away at the end of the day. I refused to wash my hands for days—I didn't want to forget the smell of the goats.

So when we returned just a few years ago, I knew a pilgrimage to the goat seter was in order. This time I went alone. I had recently been struggling with my own demons, working hard to heal old wounds, and somehow I just knew I needed to see those goats again.

Borrowing a bike from my cousin who lives just down the valley a few miles from the seter, I pedal off between steep mountains to visit the goats. When I arrive, I have to admit, I feel a little awkward. What am I expecting? A grand "welcome back" party by the goats? I honestly don't know. I just know I need to be there.

So I plop myself down on a rock, making sure to keep my bag on my back rather than on the ground—it would have been a yummy lunch for them. But I don't have to worry. A few come and check me out but then plod away, ignoring this interloper into their home. Except for one. One goat appears out of nowhere and gives me so much love it is impossible to deny. And her message to me is clear: "Thank you for working so hard to heal those old wounds. It matters."

Just like when I was a little girl, I didn't want to leave that day. But like the smell on my hands when I was eight, the memory of the message from the goat stays with me to this day.

There's a certain degree of humility required to listen to and learn from animals, birds, plants, and fish, even elements like earth, air, fire, and water. Yet are they not as intimately connected with the Divine as I am, or even more so? Didn't Jesus direct us to learn from them? What wisdom, blessing, teaching might we receive if we humble ourselves and open ourselves to their wisdom? To God's wisdom speaking through them?

Invitation:

Ask an animal what it might want to teach you. Observe and listen. What does it feel like to humble yourself to an animal's wisdom?

FIRST WEEK OF LENT: SATURDAY

Becoming Rooted, Day 16,
"Human-Centered"

I no longer speak of you as subordinates, because a subordinate doesn't
know a superior's business. Instead I call you friends, because I have
made known to you everything I have learned from Abba God.

—John 15:15

Anthropocentrism is a fancy word to describe the view that humans are above
nature....What if we began to see other creatures as necessary and as
family?...If you see the tree as a part of a family, it becomes your relative.

—Randy Woodley, *Becoming Rooted*, 43–44

Ten years ago, searching for a place to meet outdoors with a group of leaders from EcoFaith Recovery, a friend of mine and I walked along a bluff overlooking the Willamette River. From that vantage point, the river was beautiful. But the truth is, we were looking over a Superfund site. As we walked, the river herself seemed to call to us, asking us to learn more of her story and to share it with others. What resulted was The River's Lament, an imaginative ritual walk telling the story of the river in first person, as if the river were telling us her story from her perspective.

The process of listening deeply to the river challenged my internalized sense of human superiority. Why had I never learned about the river I had driven over a thousand times before? Why did I call the river an "it" when the river teems with life and water sustains all life? Water *is* life! And who else, and what else, do I continue to objectify by using "it" language or by simply failing to recognize their existence at all?

Several years ago, at a conference, I met two Indigenous women from the land known to many as Australia. As these women said farewell, they asked those of us who live in the United States to show special love and attention to any Eucalyptus trees we may see. The Eucalyptus are not just special, not just sacred; they are family to the Indigenous peoples there. And, therefore, the trees growing here are like children in exile, stolen from their homeland, separated from their families. And so these women's request was that we treat the Eucalyptus like our family because they are separated from theirs.

I thought little of this request until I went for a walk in my neighborhood, and there, just a half a block from my house, was a Eucalyptus tree. I had never really "seen" her. But suddenly, she became family. I now greet her, embrace her branches, notice how she changes with the seasons, introduce her to my walking partners.

I believe this Eucalyptus tree appreciates my care and attention. But the truth is, I am receiving much more from her than she is from me. Slowly she is helping dissolve my internalized superiority, making me more humble, more human, and more humane in the process.

Invitation:

Go for a walk in a familiar place and notice the people, plants, animals, elements that you don't usually "see." Greet them (silently or aloud) as family. Practice changing the pronoun "it" to "she/he/they" when referring to non-human living beings.

SECOND WEEK OF LENT: SUNDAY

Becoming Rooted, Day 21,
"We Are Still Here"

So YHWH fashioned an earth creature out of the clay of the earth,
and blew into its nostrils the breath of life. And the earth creature
became a living being. YHWH planted a garden to the east, in Eden...
and placed in it the earth creature that had been made. Then YHWH
caused every kind of tree, enticing to look at and good to eat, to spring
from the soil.... YHWH took the earth creature and settled it in the
garden of Eden so that it might cultivate and care for the land.

—Genesis 2:7–9a, 15

Throughout Indian country, one phrase rings true...."We are still
here!"...[G]iven the numerous attempts at cultural assimilation and
genocide that have decimated many Native American populations
by 95 percent since 1492...the statement means a lot. "We are
still here" speaks directly to the hope that remains....

—Randy Woodley, *Becoming Rooted*, 57

I didn't learn much about Native Americans in school, but I do remember learning about the Cherokee "Trail of Tears," the forced march of the Cherokee Nation in 1838 from their homelands in the Southeast to "Indian Territory" in present-day Oklahoma. The story was gut-wrenching, but it caught my attention for an additional reason. I knew that both of my great-grandfathers obtained land through the 1893 "Cherokee Strip Run," which opened part of Indian Territory, the Cherokee Outlet, to White settlement. I had heard my mom speak with pride about her grandfathers' participation in this historic event, and I had visited the farmhouse her paternal grandfather built. So when the words "Cherokee," "Indian Territory," and "Oklahoma" came up in school, my ears perked up. But my family stories had not included a Trail of Tears and theft of the Cherokee Outlet to give land to my ancestors.

Forty years after my great-grandparents began plowing up the prairie, one of the worst environmental disasters in the United States occurred: the Dust Bowl. Bad farming practices, misunderstanding of prairie ecosystems, and extended drought caused the topsoil of 24 million acres to literally blow away. The Great Plains ecosystems, managed sustainably by Native Americans for thousands of years, collapsed within two generations of White settlement.

During Lent, we are invited to wrestle with the reality of sin and the need for repentance and return to Jesus' way of healing and God's intentions for humanity. How often do we connect sin with ecological crimes or repentance with reparations? As a descendant of White settlers, I struggle with the destruction that they wrought all along the path that led to me. I wonder what authentic repentance means for me in relation to all this destruction? I am not personally responsible for what my ancestors did, but I do inherit some responsibility for the repair of the harms they participated in.

In Genesis, God creates human beings to dwell in peace with one another and with the land. God commands the first human ('adam in Hebrew) to take care of fertile soil ('adamah in Hebrew). We were created to be Earthkeepers. The descendants of the people that my people dispossessed are still here. I'm still here. What would it look like for me to follow in the way of Jesus in relation to Indigenous peoples? What would it look like for me to be the Earthkeeper God intended me to be?

Invitation:

Trace the settlement story of one line of your ancestors. What was their route across the United States? What impacts did they have on Indigenous peoples and the environments where they settled? If your ancestors were dispossessed or enslaved by White settlers, how does your family continue to be impacted by this trauma?

SECOND WEEK OF LENT: MONDAY
Becoming Rooted, Day 23,
"Place"

By the rivers of Babylon—there we sat down and there we wept when we remembered Zion. On the willows there we hung up our harps…. How could we sing the Lord's song in a foreign land?

—Psalm 137:1–2, 4, NRSV

To universalize a place is to neglect our…purpose. When we depersonalize a place, we…abuse the land. Ignoring the history of a place or treating it superficially shows extreme hubris. To treat one species in that particular environment as more important than the others displays arrogance, and we do so at our…peril.

—Randy Woodley, *Becoming Rooted*, 61–62

Where are you from? When asked that question, I say I grew up in Orlando, Florida but now live in Beaverton, Oregon. My parents came from Oklahoma and Texas. They had deep roots there, but they were not indigenous to those places. I never thought of either my parents or me as being indigenous to anywhere. So I was startled to read in the introduction to *Becoming Rooted*, "we are all indigenous, from somewhere…. Your ancestors were, at one time, all indigenous." This insight turns my world upside down. It uncovers the forgotten truth that, at some point in our ancestral history, we were all rooted and placed people.

We are proud of being a nation of immigrants, but we gloss over the loss and trauma our ancestors experienced when they were uprooted and brought here or uprooted themselves and came here. I wonder if we have become so enamored with our mobility that we have forgotten the value of truly knowing the place where we live? If we don't know our place, how can we live in harmony with the land and creatures of that place?

The ancient Hebrews were deeply rooted in their land. They knew how to survive in a harsh environment. Their faith was tied to their experience of God in particular places, not only in the Temple in Jerusalem but also in the forces of nature all around them—just read the Psalms! Psalm 137 expresses the deep grief of the people of Israel when they languished in exile in Babylon, far from their homeland.

Somewhere along the way, Christianity lost a sense of rootedness in the land as a core aspect of our faith. Our forebears became suspicious of those who experience the sacred in their landscapes and in other living creatures. They labeled those who live in intimate harmony with the land "primitive" and declared superior those who impose their will on it. They confined worship to buildings and condemned those who met God in sacred groves, springs, and mountains. Now we reap the consequences of these choices as we experience our alienation from creation in heartbreaking ways.

How do we repent from patterns of living that destroy creation's integrity and return to ways of life that restore balance and harmony? How do we connect to the place we live as a sacred place, a community of interdependent living beings? How do we meet Christ there?

Invitation:

Create a personal "land acknowledgment." What Indigenous people(s) are native to the place you live? What other species are home there? How could you enhance your sense of connection and belonging to your place during Lent? To begin learning about the original inhabitants of your place, visit https://native-land.ca/.

SECOND WEEK OF LENT: TUESDAY

Becoming Rooted, Day 22,
"Listening and Understanding"

Incline your ear, and come to me; listen, so that you may live.

—Isaiah 55:3a, NRSV

You must understand this, my beloved: let everyone be
quick to listen, slow to speak, slow to anger…

—James 1:19, NRSV

Indigenous people who are raised traditionally are taught to listen
in every situation. Like most values, this skill is caught more
than taught. Generations of people living close to the Earth
learn that listening skills are vital. When hunting…it's not just
visual observations that matter but also one's listening skills.

—Randy Woodley, *Becoming Rooted*, 59

When I was in eighth grade, I learned how to debate. The teacher divided us into teams and assigned each team one side of a controversial topic. I don't recall our topic, but I do recall the excitement of having to prepare the argument for our point of view. If we argued well enough, we would win! I don't recall ever learning in school how to actively listen to another person in order to understand their point of view. Sadly, the signs of our society's deficits in listening and empathy are everywhere. And when we don't feel heard, we just crank up the volume of our own voices. We shout when we need to get quiet and listen.

Recent events that might have generated greater capacity to listen to opposite points of view—the COVID-19 pandemic, the murder of George Floyd—have, for some, had the opposite effect. This is at least partially due to the lack of effective leadership from our elected and appointed officials and even from church leaders. But our Bible is full of admonitions to listen—to God, to other people, and to the whole chorus of creation (Ps. 19). Every authentic wisdom tradition teaches some version of James's exhortation to "be quick to listen, slow to speak."

People living close to the land—Indigenous peoples and others living from the land—know that listening to the natural world is critical to survival. My cousin tells the story of watching our grandpa step out on the farmhouse porch and quietly survey the sky. After several minutes, he would confidently predict what kind of weather was coming. He was almost always right! Some people have learned how to listen to other people with the kind of attention that Indigenous people and farmers bring to the natural world. Can you imagine the difference it would make if our schools, churches, businesses, and governments modeled and taught these kinds of active listening skills?

Active, empathic listening is hard work. It requires us to check our egos, stop rehearsing our lines, and put ourselves in another's shoes. The reward is not as immediate as the exhilarating feeling of winning, but it is much more gratifying over the long run. When we really listen to God, to our fellow humans created in God's image, and to our companion species in the web of life, we might lose an argument, but we gain the world!

Invitation:

Identify one or two new ways that you can practice actively listening to BIPOC people (Black, Indigenous, People of Color) during Lent; for example, subscribe to a podcast or watch films or TV shows written and produced by BIPOC people; invite a BIPOC friend or co-worker to coffee to deepen your relationship.

SECOND WEEK OF LENT: WEDNESDAY

Becoming Rooted, Day 24,
"The Circle"

You have heard it said, "Love your neighbor—but hate your enemy."
But I tell you, love your enemies and pray for your persecutors. This
will prove that you are children of God. For God makes the sun
rise on bad and good alike; God's rain falls on the just and unjust....
Therefore be perfect [complete], as Abba God in heaven is perfect.

—Matthew 5:43–45, 48

One model of understanding our relationship to everything
is a simple symbol used among Native Americans: the circle.
The harmony way of living is often referred to symbolically as
a circle....Among Native Americans, the harmony way is less
like a philosophy and more like a whole way of being.

—Randy Woodley, *Becoming Rooted*, 63

The way of Jesus, the teachings of Buddha, and the wisdom of Indigenous peoples share this in common: a fundamental understanding of the interdependence of all living things. Everything is connected; nothing exists in isolation. For complex reasons, Indigenous peoples the world over still perceive "the circle of life" while non-Indigenous peoples strive to live in a world of human-centric straight lines (progress!). As a result, it's true, as Randy Woodley says, that Indigenous cultures prize harmony, balance, sustainability, and sharing more highly than Western cultures.

When I was working on my dissertation on sustainable development, I learned this firsthand. I traveled up to the Akwesasne Mohawk Reservation on the US-Canada border to meet with leaders in the Haudenosaunee Environmental Task Force. I had the incredible opportunity to interview Chief Jake Swamp, a legendary Mohawk leader.

Chief Swamp told me a story remarkably similar to the one that Randy Woodley tells in his reflection entitled "Berries" in *Becoming Rooted*. He said that when he was a child, he learned that whenever he went out to pick berries, he could never take them all. He always had to leave some for the birds and animals because they are our relatives. In fact, the Haudenosaunee teach that we are the "youngest child" in creation. We need all the other beings in the web of life more than they need us! Can you imagine how the story of White settlement in this continent would have unfolded differently if settlers had perceived all the original inhabitants of this continent as our relatives?

Today, we face a crisis. The web of life is unraveling. Whether due to our addiction to fossil fuels, vaccine hoarding by rich nations, callous exclusion of refugees seeking sanctuary, or political hate speech, our world is speeding toward social and ecological breakdown. But there is another way. Jesus taught with his life and words that we are all children of the same God, subject to the same ultimate conditions of life and death. Jesus' way of nonviolent love, the harmony way of Indigenous peoples, and all other authentic faiths point in the same direction—treat others as we would be treated, respect the web of life that supports us. This is not just a moral imperative; it's the way we survive the coming storm. As Lutheran ecological ethicist Larry Rasmussen sums it up, "it's life together now, or not at all."

Invitation:

Visualize a person or creature that you struggle to tolerate. Trace ways that your well-being and theirs are connected. What do you both need? What kinds of suffering do you share? Visualize this person or creature suffering and ask God to allow empathy to arise within you. Pray for their well-being.

SECOND WEEK OF LENT: THURSDAY

Becoming Rooted, Day 26, "Intentional Relationship"

The truth of the matter is, unless a grain of wheat falls on the ground and dies, it remains only a single grain; but if it dies, it yields a rich harvest. If you love your life you'll lose it; if you hate your life in this world you'll keep it for eternal life. Anyone who wants to work for me must follow in my footsteps.

—John 12:24–26a

With my first bite of food, I think about what I am eating. I understand the sacrifice made by the plant or the animal to give me life. My life is connected to their death. There is a sacred relationship between myself and the food I eat.

—Randy Woodley, *Becoming Rooted*, 67–68

During the COVID-19 lockdown in 2020, I had a lot more time to work on my spiritual practice. I've long struggled with staying alert with my eyes closed in meditation or centering prayer, so I decided to move my spiritual practice outdoors. My wife calls me a nature mystic. When I'm outdoors, I'm mesmerized by the world around me. As I get older, I'm only falling more deeply in love with the natural world. My wife knows not to take it personally if I interrupt her on one of our walks to point out a particularly beautiful tree, cloud formation, or bird. I delight in God's creations. So I began to practice open-eyed meditation in our backyard: simply bringing my attention to the life all around me—the sights, sounds, smells—and opening my inner eye to see the God who dwells in matter. I'm never disappointed. I try not to expect insights, but sometimes they come.

One fresh morning, as I sat quietly, I noticed an array of sounds that I can only call eating sounds. The birds were pecking at the bark of the Scots Pine tree, and other sounds I didn't recognize were likely the sounds of insects eating their breakfast. Munch, munch, munch. And suddenly, something clicked for me. Oh my God, I thought, the world is always feeding! The world is always eating and being eaten. The world is always COMMUNING!

Real mystics know that sacraments don't only happen in church. Real mystics know that the world itself is sacrament—a visible sign of an invisible grace—an ongoing revelation of the WORD made FLESH. When Jesus offers his body as bread for the world, he offers us a portal into the mind-blowing realization that everything that is, is God enfleshed. For Christians, Jesus is simply the human revelation of the God who feeds the world from her own body.

Feeding is a sacrificial act of love. Ask any mother nursing her infant. Jesus' desire to nourish the world to eternal life led to the cross. Many Indigenous people believe that animals and plants willingly sacrifice their lives to nourish other life forms, including humans. To maintain the balance, humans need to offer sacrifices to the spirits of these animals in thanksgiving for their sacrifice. I don't understand these mysteries, but I do know that God created a world in which love and sacrifice, eating and being eaten, are inescapable. Can I see God in all that feeds me? Can I share the life of God in all that I feed?

Invitation:

When have you loved another sacrificially? Identify five beings that are making a sacrifice for your well-being today.

SECOND WEEK OF LENT: FRIDAY
Becoming Rooted, Day 28,
"Paw Prints"

And God said to me, "My grace is sufficient for you, for power
is perfected in weakness." Most gladly, therefore, I would rather
boast about my weaknesses, that the power of Christ may dwell
in me. So I am content with weakness, with mistreatment,
with distress, with persecutions and difficulties for the sake of
Christ; when I am powerless, it is then that I am strong.

—2 Corinthians 12:9–10

Is there an obstacle in your life too large for you to
handle? Accepting defeat and asking for help is sometimes
wiser than what we mistake for courage.

—Randy Woodley, *Becoming Rooted*, 72

During Lent, we stretch to grasp the most obscure mystery of the Christian faith—the way of the cross. The testimony of Scripture that Jesus' way of the cross is also the way to abundant life is completely counterintuitive. Even now, after years of being a pastor, something in me cringes at the language of 2 Corinthians 12. Yet the gospels and epistles insist on this one point—that the meek inherit the Earth.

I doubt that the way of the cross can be taught. I suspect it can only be learned through experience. Like the gigantic Kodiak bear that Randy Woodley nearly encountered in Alaska, sometimes we come up against obstacles that we cannot overcome on our own—like the challenge of climate change. When human beings face a threat that's beyond our control, we often have one of three reactions: "fight," "flight," or "freeze." Some people fight the facts by fostering denial that climate change is happening. Others flee into avoidance and distractions. Many feel paralyzed by helplessness and grief. Within each of these three responses, there can also remain an unexamined confidence, hope, or fantasy that human technology will save us. That simple lifestyle changes will save us. That big policy changes will save us. But, as Audre Lorde warned, "the master's tools will never dismantle the master's house."

I wonder how we might handle the climate crisis differently if we grasped the truth Jesus' way of the cross reveals: only when we release our pretensions to superiority and, in one sense, accept defeat, will we find our way to the other side of this climate crucifixion. But this is no counsel of despair. For what needs defeating is not the human spirit, not hope for our children's future, but a worldview that sees people as separate from creation, that assumes human ingenuity is more powerful than Earth's limits. Such a worldview makes an idol of human power.

This idolatrous faith in human *power over* creation is what must be nailed to the cross for life as we know it to continue. Only when we accept our place in creation's web as humble caretakers, not masters, can Earth's healing begin. And ours as well. Only when we *seek help* from Creator and other creatures will Earth's harmony be restored. Jesus knew this, Indigenous peoples know it still, and the cosmic and risen Christ who dwells within us whispers it continually, for those who have ears to hear.

Invitation:

Have you experienced the way of the cross? When have you needed to ask for help? How did you experience God's power working through your weakness? Spend some time with your journal or sketch pad reflecting on these questions.

SECOND WEEK OF LENT: SATURDAY

Becoming Rooted, Day 30,
"My Porch Swing"

Then YHWH answered Job from the heart of the storm: Who is
this obscuring my plans with such ignorant words? Hitch up your
belt like the fighter you are; now I will ask the questions and you
will answer me! Where were you when I created the earth? If you
know the answer, tell me! Who decided its size? Do you know? Who
stretched the measuring line across it? Into what foundations were
its pillars sunk? Who laid the cornerstone while all the choruses
of morning stars sang and the heavenly court shouted for joy?

—Job 38:1–7

A filbert does not want to be a tree. It sends from its roots many
small trees,…[as] hedges might wander.…[A]ttempts to tame these
trees may be part of the problem: by trimming them down to
one trunk, we try to make them into something they are not.

—Randy Woodley, *Becoming Rooted,* 75–76

Filbert (hazelnut) orchards are everywhere in Oregon's Willamette Valley. When I first moved to Oregon, I wondered what the rows upon rows of neatly planted trees were that I drove by so frequently. The Willamette Valley is the breadbasket of Oregon. I have often been in awe of the variety of crops that range through this beautiful valley that extends roughly from Portland to Eugene. When my imagination runs away from me on certain drives through the country, when the fields look particularly bucolic in the soft sunlight, I feel as though I've stumbled into the Garden of Eden. Yet in his reflection in *Becoming Rooted*, "My Porch Swing," Randy Woodley jolts me back to reality. These filbert orchards and all of the other gorgeous green crops of different hues are far from Eden's paradise. Although Oregon ranks sixth in the nation in the number of acres under certified organic cultivation, many conventional farms continue to employ unsustainable industrial agricultural practices.

What happens to filberts, forced to grow against their nature as a single-trunked tree, is paradigmatic of Western culture. Mostly, we want to bend nature into forms that fit our vision of beauty or functionality and further our agenda for profit. So I have a confession to make. A couple of years ago, my wife and I planted two Vine Maples in our backyard. Now, if you google Acer circinatum, you will see that Vine Maples are classified as both shrubs and trees. But you see, we wanted small trees, not large bushes, so we were advised that we should prune the plant the following year to encourage a single trunk and remove competitors. This past year, on several occasions, I eyed those Vine Maples. I contemplated taking out the pruning shears and lopping off the branches whose arms stick out at crooked angles, their elbows jostling for space. Thankfully, I could not bring myself to do it.

The early voyageurs called the Vine Maple "Bois de diable" (Tree of the Devil) because it obstructed their view. In the Western mind, thwarting human will is the devil's work. But there's hope that perspectives are changing. Oregon State University's Department of Horticulture describes the Vine Maple as having "ethereal horizontal grace" and warns that this unique feature is lost when it is heavily pruned. May we all join Indigenous peoples and enlightened horticulturalists in valuing the ethereal horizontal (and dare we say, divine) grace of wild things.

Invitation:

This Lent, practice "untaming" a small corner of your world. Maybe it's letting a plant follow nature's course. Maybe it's co-existing with spiders (or catching and releasing these beneficial insects). Maybe it's freeing your mind from dominant culture blinders. What can you let run wild?

THIRD WEEK OF LENT: SUNDAY
Becoming Rooted, Day 31,
"Lived Experience"

But turn to the animals, and let them teach you; the birds of the air will tell you the truth. Listen to the plants of the earth, and learn from them; let the fish of the sea become your teachers. Who among all these does not know that the hand of YHWH has done this? In God's hand is the soul of every living thing; in God's hand is the breath of all humankind.

—Job 12:7–10

Indigenous peoples value lived experience over dry knowledge. In Indian country, true knowledge is not so much about facts as it is about gaining an understanding or even a revelation from creation, a dream, or an experience.

—Randy Woodley, *Becoming Rooted*, 79

A few months before my dad passed away, we sat in his hospital room, and he asked me a very profound question: "Jimmy, what have you learned from me?" Dad's question caught me off guard, but my answers rolled off my tongue like the waves that rolled on the beaches of Lahaina, where he grew up. Answers like "the Spirit of Aloha, treat all people with dignity, 'ohana ("family" in Hawaiian) is everything" left my mouth and heart. As I shared, a smile crawled across my dad's face. The things I learned from dad were not simply words of wisdom but what I saw in how he lived his life.

My dad was a recreational therapist at the Oregon State Hospital, the same hospital where *One Flew Over the Cuckoo's Nest* was filmed. As children, it was always an interesting adventure visiting dad at work, going on camping trips or riding with the patients on the bus and spending the day at the Oregon State Fair.

When I was in junior high, my brother and I were with my dad in a grocery store when a loud and boisterous individual started shouting from across the store repeatedly, "Hey Windy, is that you?" The shouting was embarrassing, but even more embarrassing was how he shuffled his contorted body and flailing arms across the store towards my dad. My brother and I stepped away from my dad, not wanting to be guilty by association at this spectacle unfolding. But my dad walked toward that individual, and when they got close enough, they hugged. They talked and laughed for what seemed like an eternity. They hugged again, and my dad turned and started walking toward us when the patient started waving and yelled out, "Hey Windy, it was really good to see you again!" My dad smiled, turned around, and said, "Same here." Then dad told my brother and me, "He used to be a patient at the state hospital," and nothing more.

It was by watching our dad in his encounters and interactions with the patients from the Oregon State Hospital—people whom society considers rejects, losers, loners, and the lost—that we learned the importance of treating all people with dignity. When I think back on the things that I learned from my dad, the really important things I remember that I'm passing down to my children and *mo'opunas* ("grandchildren" in Hawaiian), it was not his words of wisdom, but the wisdom in how he lived each day.

Invitation:

My Hawaiian ancestors knew the Uncreated Creator long before missionaries arrived, through God's actions and activities in creation. Creation points to God and God's righteousness. What have you learned from the Creator through a bird's song, majestic trees, the sunrise, or the changing seasons?

THIRD WEEK OF LENT: MONDAY

Becoming Rooted, Day 32,
"Married to the Land"

The earth and everything on it—the world and all who live in it—belong
to YHWH. YHWH built it on the deep waters, laying its foundations in the
ocean depths. Who has the right to ascend to YHWH's mountain? Who
is allowed to enter YHWH's holy place? Those whose hands are clean and
whose hearts are pure, who do not worship idols, or make false promises.

—Psalm 24:1–4

How do people become married to the land? What intimacies
of love and commitment and daily relationship emerge?
The degree to which we are willing to spend time alone
with the land may determine the level of intimacy.

—Randy Woodley, *Becoming Rooted*, 81

As we got closer to the sacred Queen's Bath near Kalapana in Hawai'i, I could tell by the cautious excitement in my grandparents' voices that we were about to see something amazing and beautiful. Whenever we would visit from the Pacific Northwest, we would see and hear stories about our ancestral history, culture, and various sacred places that were important to Hawaiians. Before arriving at the various destinations, we were instructed on protocols and attitudes as we entered certain areas or walked the land. The cautious excitement in my grandparents' voices was a mixture of understanding the importance and sacredness of the protocols and the excitement for them of showing us the Queen's Bath. As we followed our grandparents through lush tropical greens, the quiet sacredness was abruptly interrupted with hushes and laughter just ahead of us. Suddenly, four visitors from the mainland, naked and clutching their clothes, rushed past us. I immediately saw it on the face of my grandparents; their countenance went from sacred to subdued as if they had been personally violated, which they were. These four guests to Hawai'i decided to go skinny-dipping in one of the most sacred pools on the island. When we arrived at the Queen's Bath, my grandparents stood silently grieving—that entire space was grieving. Nothing much was said. Nothing needed to be said.

For Native Hawaiians, the land is not a commodity. It is a relative that is cared for and who, in turn, cares for us. The Hawaiian word for land is *'aina*, which also encompasses the ocean, rivers, flora and all of creation. "*Malama 'aina*" is a phrase that reminds us of our responsibility to care for the land and properly manage the gifts the *'aina* provides. Indigenous peoples see ourselves as caretakers and stewards of the land, the Creator's land. Indigenous peoples had no concept of owning land, which could be equated to owning a cousin, nephew, niece, or any other relative. The grief on my grandparents' faces that day at the Queen's Bath is still with me today. I often ask myself living here in the Pacific Northwest, "Am I being a good guest on the host people's land? Am I treating the *'aina* with the care and respect that makes me a good guest, especially among our Native American hosts?"

Invitation:

The Uncreated Creator gave Native Americans the responsibility to care for and properly manage this *'aina* they call Turtle Island. They are our hosts. How might you get to know the host people in your area and hear their story of the *'aina*? What can you learn from the host people about the Creator and the gifts of creation?

THIRD WEEK OF LENT: TUESDAY

Becoming Rooted, Day 33,
"Caretakers"

Praise YHWH from the earth, you sea creatures and ocean depths,
lightning and hail, snow and mist, and storm winds that fulfill
God's word, mountains and all hills, fruit trees and all cedars,
wild animals and all cattle, small animals and flying birds!

—Psalm 148:7–10

If the help of Indigenous peoples is to be sought, actions are needed
now. Confession of the wrongs done to Indigenous peoples around the
world must include acts of restitution, restoration, and empowerment.

—Randy Woodley, *Becoming Rooted*, 84

When my Auntie Pa'iaina was a young girl living in Hilo, Hawai'i, she was so excited for Sunday School and to share the verse she was given to memorize. She was especially excited because she had some insight that brought her verse to life. The excitement was building as each child shared their verse. Finally, it was Auntie's turn. She stood proudly and proclaimed, "Jesus said, 'I am the *poi* of life,'" but she was surprised by her Sunday School teacher's response. Her teacher flicked her on the lips with her finger and sternly replied, "That's wrong. Jesus is not the *poi* of life; Jesus is the bread of life." My aunt was so embarrassed. *Poi* is the byproduct of kalo or taro when it is pounded. Kalo is part of the Hawaiian creation story and is referred to as the root of life. The stalk that grows from the kalo is called *oha*, from which the word *'ohana* (family) is derived. Kalo reminds Hawaiians that we are related to not only the kalo but all of creation. *Poi* has also been an important staple that has sustained Hawaiians for centuries. So when Auntie said, "Jesus is the *poi* of life," she knew what she was talking about.

Indigenous peoples have been categorized as uncivilized, primitive, and uneducated. The Doctrine of Discovery was a decree used by European Christians to dehumanize Indigenous peoples by stating that any lands not inhabited by Christians justified the seizure of those lands and the enslavement or genocide of Indigenous peoples. The Doctrine of Discovery was foundational and justified the colonization in the United States, the illegal stealing, and the intentional genocide of Native peoples who had lived here for over 15,000 years. The Doctrine of Discovery became part of US federal law and continues to be used to dispossess Native peoples of their land.

The truth is that Indigenous peoples knew the Creator long before the missionaries arrived with their Bible. Throughout Scripture, especially in the Psalms, the land, the kalo, rivers, oceans, birds, wild animals, cattle, and small creatures testify to the Creator's presence. Most Indigenous cultures acknowledge the Uncreated Creator. Native Americans have lived as hosts on this land in partnership with creation for over 15,000 years. Americans have occupied this land for less than three hundred years, and you don't have to look far to see we are in trouble. Maybe it's time to decolonize Christianity and learn from Indigenous peoples what Creator has taught them, like what my Auntie knew: Jesus is the *poi* of life.

Invitation:

Read about the Doctrine of Discovery (doctrineofdiscovery.org) and learn about the injustices that need to be corrected. Read a book written by a Native American or Indigenous theologian.

THIRD WEEK OF LENT: WEDNESDAY

Becoming Rooted, Day 34,
"Ethnic Identity"

After that, I saw before me an immense crowd without number, from every nation, tribe, people and language. They stood in front of the throne and the Lamb, dressed in long white robes and holding palm branches.

—Revelation 7:9

Whatever way one comes at their own Indigenous identity, each person has much to add to the cultural splendor that has been given as a birthright to the people of that particular land.

—Randy Woodley, *Becoming Rooted*, 86

My dad was from Lahaina, Maui, my mom was from Hilo, Hawai'i, and they both moved to Salem, Oregon, to attend college. For economic reasons, they decided to make Salem their "home." Before I started attending elementary school, I remember my mom instructing me to make sure I dressed nicely, combed my hair, treated others respectfully, and presented myself well because "people will look at you differently." Her most important instructions, however, would follow: "Be proud you're Hawaiian." I never forgot my mom's words and the seriousness with which she spoke them. My parents wanted us to delight in our heritage and be proud of our Indigenous identity, even though we were an ocean apart from our 'ohana (family) and 'aina (motherland). We lived out the cultural lessons, stories, and values that were passed down from my parents' 'ohana and kupuna (elders) through food, music, hula/dance, stories and legends, protocols, faith, and ancestral lineage. I am grateful for the beauty, kindness, and Aloha my Hawaiian culture has contributed in blessing other cultures and societies it has come in contact with—locally and globally. (I hesitate to translate "Aloha" because of the breadth of its meaning, but "unconditional love" would be a starting point.)

Despite the beauty of our culture, our Hawaiian history is filled with stories of Western colonialism trying to erase our Hawaiian culture and the Hawaiian people. When a close friend of mine became a follower of Jesus, the pastor who prayed with him said, "You're a Christian now. You are no longer Hawaiian."

Everyone is indigenous with a beautiful and magnificent ancestral heritage. What is your indigenous ancestral heritage? What does your ancestral heritage and culture have to contribute to bless other cultures? Because all peoples have been created in God's image, we all have something to contribute to other cultures. When I read Revelation 7 and its vision of the multitude from every nation and tribe, I see all indigenous peoples bringing the best of what their culture has to offer and placing it before the Lamb for everyone to appreciate and enjoy.

Invitation:

Consider reading and investigating more about your ancestral indigenous identity. Consider taking a DNA test. If you can identify ancestral indigenous roots, look for ways to share and celebrate your indigenous identity with others and how it reflects the Creator. Be proud and remember that you are wonderfully and beautifully made.

THIRD WEEK OF LENT: THURSDAY
Becoming Rooted, Day 36,
"Making Relatives"

But Ruth said to her, "Please don't ask me to leave you and turn away from
your company. I swear to you: Where you go, I will go; where you lodge,
I will lodge. Your people will be my people, and your God, my God."

—Ruth 1:16–17a

In the Indian way, adoption is more than just a symbolic
gesture; it is a necessary means to include others. Everyone
in the tribe has a role and a relative status.

—Randy Woodley, *Becoming Rooted*, 90

Thanks to the Disney movie, *Lilo and Stitch*, the word *'ohana* has become a household word. If you haven't seen the movie (spoiler alert) Lilo says, "*'Ohana* means family, family means no one gets left behind or forgotten." *'Ohana* goes beyond one's bloodline. *'Ohana* is belonging and sharing in the responsibilities of your *kuleana*. *Kuleana* is the reciprocal relationship between the person who is responsible and the thing or person they are responsible for. When our children were young, they wanted an allowance for doing various chores around the house—we said no. The chores were part of being in the Sequeira *'ohana*; it was part of their *kuleana*. Still pressing for an allowance, we said if they wanted an allowance, they would need to start paying rent.

I did not discover until after an aunty passed, my dad's oldest sister, that she was *hanai* (adopted). When children were *hanai* there was no paperwork involved. Children were *hanai* if family members were childless or having difficulties getting pregnant. Children were also *hanai* to grandparents as a means to learn and perpetuate Hawaiian culture. Most importantly, when a child was *hanai* they were fully a part of the *'ohana* without the stigma of being adopted.

Growing up in the Pacific Northwest, an ocean away from my parents' *'ohana*, we were blessed to be *hanai* by many of my parents' friends from Hawai'i, and we didn't miss out on growing up with many aunties, uncles, and cousins. Our Hawaiian *'ohana* in the Pacific Northwest played as significant a role in our upbringing as our *'ohana* in Hawai'i did. *'Ohana* isn't restricted to place or ethnicity. Randy and Edith Woodley are yet another example of *'ohana*, where my children refer to them as Uncle Randy and Aunty Edith.

'Ohana is much more than leaving no one behind or forgetting anyone; *'ohana* is belonging and sharing in the responsibilities of your *kuleana*. The relationship between Naomi and Ruth is a beautiful example of *'ohana*.

Invitation:

Because there is one Creator, we are all relatives. We are all *'ohana*. What can you do to make the stranger or those on the fringes a relative?

THIRD WEEK OF LENT: FRIDAY
Becoming Rooted, Day 37,
"Pow Wow"

I will joyfully exult in YHWH, who is the joy of my soul! My God clothed me with a robe of deliverance and wrapped me in a mantle of justice, the way a bridegroom puts on a turban and a bride bedecks herself with jewels.

—Isaiah 61:10

A Pow Wow is a social event where Native American cultural splendor is displayed at its finest. Pow Wows can be found in all fifty states and nearly all Canadian provinces, and they are public events to which everyone in the community is invited.

—Randy Woodley, *Becoming Rooted*, 91

It's all about the event, whether worshiping on Sunday morning (or whenever we worship) or attending a luau. We show up, are entertained, and go home. Isaiah tells us there's more to worship than just showing up.

Most people think the luau is a delicious meal, wonderful music and beautiful women and men dancing the hula. But actually, there are three movements making up the luau. The first movement is preparing the meal. Grandparents, aunties, uncles, cousins and children work together to prepare the feast, and as the meal is being prepared, family stories are being shared. We call it "talk story." Sometimes the stories might sound like reruns, but in an oral tradition, culture repetition helps in remembering. I discovered that in the process of hearing a story over and over, the story becomes my story, passed on by my *kupuna* (elders).

There are also rites of passage, like when a *kupuna* places a knife in your hand and teaches you how to cut the vegetable, meat, or fish. When given a family recipe, that also is a rite of passage. Another rite of passage is being allowed to sit through the night babysitting the kalua pig cooking in the *imu* (underground oven). The first movement concludes by getting the tables set up and the place decorated.

The second movement of the luau is sharing the spirit of hospitality— serving well and making sure everyone is getting plenty of good food and having a good time. When it comes to the entertainment, it just happens and is free-flowing—musicians, singers, and hula dancers sharing their gifts. At my daughter's wedding, there was no Hawaiian program planned, we just let it happen, and the music and hula dancing lasted for almost an hour.

The third movement of the luau is where everyone helps clean up and put things away. The unspoken motto during cleanup is that no one leaves alone—everyone stays until the work/cleaning is done. We've hosted large parties at our house, and it's always been our Hawaiian 'ohana who stuck around and helped us clean up. The three movements of a luau build and deepen relationship, perpetuate our Hawaiian culture by passing down and learning stories, and give us the opportunity to share the spirit by blessing others. While the luau event is always amazing, the richness and blessing of being involved in all three movements of a luau are even more amazing.

Invitation:

Take time today to learn of another culture's celebrations and ceremonies. Instead of just showing up to the event, see how you might get involved with all three movements of the celebration. Remember, the Creator gifted each culture with their celebrations and ceremonies.

THIRD WEEK OF LENT: SATURDAY

Becoming Rooted, Day 38,
"Sweet Potatoes, Chicken, Stars, and a Blue Moon"

Some went down to the sea in ships, plying their trade
across the ocean; they too saw the works of YHWH,
the wonders that God worked on the Deep!

—Psalm 107:23–24

The Polynesians, especially those of Hawaii, have always been great
navigators. They relied on these same stars and others to take them across
one-third of the Earth's surface, or what we now call the Pacific Ocean.

—Randy Woodley, *Becoming Rooted*, 94

Family road trips were kept to about sixty miles. Within sixty miles, we could visit family and friends, go to the Oregon Coast, fish at Detroit Lake, and drive to the Portland Airport to fly to Hawai'i to visit our *'ohana*. We teased that dad had a chain hooked to the bumper of the car that was sixty miles long—my dad just didn't like driving far. Ironically our Hawaiian ancestors left the Marquesas Islands on a 2,000-mile canoe trip and settled on an uninhabited island we now call Hawai'i in 400 AD. The Polynesian migration by sea originated out of Taiwan around 3000 BC.

Polynesian voyagers were called wayfinders. Wayfinding was a unique art of navigating without the use of instruments but taking cues from creation and using the stars, sun, moon, clouds, currents, and seabirds. There was a strong belief the first settlers to Hawai'i came from South America because the ocean currents move east to west, and so they simply caught a ride. Research has revealed, however, that Polynesian voyagers sailed *to* South America and returned home. And once the Hawaiian Islands were settled and established, the Hawaiian peoples stayed put, the ocean becoming a major highway for trading with other islands like Tahiti or for returning to visit *'ohana*.

Finding and populating the islands of the Pacific was not accidental, and while the exact location may not have been known at the time, these early wayfinders set sail with the knowledge that they would find land. My Hawaiian ancestors set sail into the mystery with the Indigenous wisdom of their ancestors to guide them. Indigenous wisdom proved for centuries that there was something to be found on the other side of mystery. The passing down of Indigenous wisdom and putting it into practice helped sustain our people for centuries and, in the words of Captain Kirk, "To go where no man has gone before." My *kupuna* (elder) shared this: "We are the descendants of our ancestors and the ancestors of our descendants." Indigenous wisdom is to be passed along and shared for the good of all peoples and not hoarded.

We live in mystery, and the greatest mystery of all is death and what is on the other side. I believe that what I've learned from my ancestors, creation, Jesus, and Scriptures, is that on the other side of the great mystery, something beautiful awaits.

Invitation:

The Uncreated Creator has gifted you with talents and wisdom passed down to you from someone you trust and appreciate. Find someone to pass along the talent or wisdom given to you. As you have received well, give well.

FOURTH WEEK OF LENT: SUNDAY

Becoming Rooted, Day 41, "Living With Nature"

Look at the birds in the sky. They don't sow or reap, they gather nothing into barns, yet our God in heaven feeds them....Learn a lesson from the way the wildflowers grow. They don't work; they don't spin. Yet I tell you, not even Solomon in full splendor was arrayed like one of these.

—Matthew 6:26a, 28b–29

The settlers wanted to live *on* the land, but the host people lived *with* the land. Living on the land means objectifying the land and natural resources and being shortsighted concerning the future. Living with the land means respecting the natural balance.

—Randy Woodley, *Becoming Rooted*, 102

A certain meadow caught my attention about two years ago. It lies adjacent to some trails I walk a few times per week—often in the mornings or around dusk. I've been particularly drawn to the milkweed and their relationship to monarch butterflies.

I observed the milkweed plants coming up as shoots in the early spring before they sprouted their iconic leaves and seed pods. Their presence means an available food supply for the monarch larvae. Throughout the rest of the year, even through fluctuating temperatures, flooding, or drought, this meadow lives as a spectacle of biodiversity with a heavy presence of pollinators that we all need for food to grow. At times the milkweed's fluffy seeds float around the meadow like a light snow until the plants eventually dry out and decay into the soil.

The east coast migration of monarch butterflies typically takes four generations to travel from Mexico to Canada and back. Three generations to get north, each living only a few weeks and dying after laying their eggs. The fourth generation lives longer and needs to in order to make the long journey back south to lay their eggs. Then the next generation starts their northward trajectory. I'm in awe of their intergenerational intelligence. I appreciate the need to protect and reestablish wetlands in my region, increasing milkweed and other plants that our pollinators need. Many such pollinators are under threat, and if we don't actively restore wetlands, there will soon be no more milkweed, and subsequently, no more monarch butterflies. That would have a catastrophic effect on our ecosystem, including food production for human beings.

The Creator gives us these gifts, and they can teach us about the relatedness of all things. When we take in the beauty of a single monarch butterfly and its intricate patterns and colors, we get a glimpse of the deep inherent intelligence that these creatures carry across generations. Understanding their interrelatedness with other species like the milkweed and how their relationship connects to our own food supply reveals that we, too, play an integral part in this interrelated intergenerational web of beauty. Lent can be a time of allowing our attention, our spirits, and our bodies to be re-centered and reconnected to creation and Creator.

Invitation:

Find ways to spend time in wonder with the land today. Go to a park or scenic vista, or your own yard. Select a species that you can commit to observing regularly for a year. Start practices like reading about the species, what threats they face, and how they directly connect to your own life.

FOURTH WEEK OF LENT: MONDAY

Becoming Rooted, Day 42,
"Myths that Tell Our Story"

You, however, are a "chosen people, a royal priesthood, a consecrated
nation, a people set apart" to sing the praises of the One who called
you out of the darkness into the wonderful, divine light. Once you
were "not a people," but now you are the people of God; once
there was "no mercy for you," but now you have found mercy.

—1 Peter 2:9–10

America tells a story about itself.... a story based on freedom,
equality, opportunity, and fairness. These imagined values spin a
narrative that America is *the* place where the divine story uniquely
comes together with the human story and unfolds as divine
providence. We could call it the myth of American exceptionalism.

—Randy Woodley, *Becoming Rooted*, 103

You can learn a lot about a people by listening to the stories they tell about themselves. These stories often get at the most deeply held values of the group as well as the place that they come from. Some stories resonate so deeply that they take on a life of their own as they are shared across generations. Communal stories shape worldview, culture, and behavior.

Peoples who maintain intergenerational relatedness to a land develop stories of being formed by those lands, including particular plants and animals of that place. These stories often tell about the beginning of the world, illustrating moral lessons, worldviews, and purpose. Other stories live as cautionary tales, illustrating things like when a people got it wrong, were corrected, and thus carried on specific ecological practices.

The United States formed itself at a time when some particular ethnic Europeans hatched a substitute story that would be told over the generations about "Americans" and would grow to include holidays, songs, and pledges of allegiance. It would become a distinct nation from Europe and, in the minds of Americans, would nullify any prior commitments made to Indigenous peoples—referred to in the Declaration of Independence as "merciless Indian savages." This story would validate their own power over the land by expanding their colonies/states, thereby replacing the stories of any peoples who lived on those lands. Their story wouldn't be about how to live well on a particular land; it would be a dream about freedom.

The irony of the American dream has always been its duplicity. The opportunities for social mobility without oppressive government have always legally been limited to some and denied to others. As Dr. Woodley claims, the American dream has been an Indigenous nightmare. The wealth gained by White people has been at the expense of Indigenous peoples as well as Black folks, women, and other systematically marginalized groups. Most mainstream opportunities for education, employment, shopping, worship, etc., still have legal or unconscious race-based barriers to entry, belonging, and promotion.

Invitation:

What are some intergenerational stories you have been told or that you continue to tell about who you belong to as a people? About the lands in which you now live? About what it means to be an American? Ask an elder in your life to tell you a story and listen to what they say.

FOURTH WEEK OF LENT: TUESDAY

Becoming Rooted, Day 43,
"Doctrine of Discovery"

The Eleven made their way to Galilee,…At the sight of the risen Christ they fell down in homage, though some doubted what they were seeing. Jesus came forward and addressed them in these words: "All authority has been given me both in heaven and on earth; go, therefore, and make disciples of all the nations. Baptize them in the name of Abba God, and of the Only Begotten, and of the Holy Spirit. Teach them to carry out everything I have commanded you. And know that I am with you always, even until the end of the world!"

—Matthew 28:16–20

For more than five centuries, Indigenous peoples across the world had their land, labor, and resources stolen and were systematically denied their human rights. What made this massive theft conceivable to the settlers who enacted the violence? The answer: the doctrine of discovery and the international laws based on it.

—Randy Woodley, *Becoming Rooted*, 105

The Doctrine of Discovery lives as the theological groundwork for legal European global dominance over non-Christian lands and people. It has shaped the Western church's interpretation of Scripture since the colonial era. And it continues to shape Christian faith traditions, underpinning a purpose of accruing wealth/power/influence and a mission of land dispossession and cultural sameness.

By the end of the fifteenth century, Christian Europeans began granting themselves, as Christians, the legal right to colonize lands outside of Europe. Whether the missionaries and explorers had the purest of hearts and noblest of intentions or were desperate European peasants fleeing certain death to build a better life, the primary beneficiaries of their collective actions were European Christians and their White descendants. On the flip side, the negative impacts came heaviest upon the Indigenous peoples of these lands and the peoples stolen from Africa and their descendants. The former would be dehumanized, removed, assimilated, or eradicated. The latter would be used as subhumanized, unfree labor—both strategies to multiply the wealth, power, and influence of White Christian men. The legal and church systems built on the Doctrine of Discovery continue to maintain the same essential status quo.

As a White Christian settler, receiving multiple privileges has never required my active support. For White supremacist systems to go on working, they don't actually need any effort from me. In order to continue, White Christian supremacy just needs us not to fight it actively. As individuals, as communities of faith, and in concert with the voices of those who are still marginalized, we have to actively be involved in dismantling those oppressive systems of privilege and exclusion. We need to repudiate the Doctrine of Discovery.

Invitation:

Read *Unsettling Truths: The Ongoing, Dehumanizing Legacy of the Doctrine of Discovery,* by Mark Charles and Soong-Chan Rah. Look into groups who are actively dismantling the Doctrine of Discovery (doctrineofdiscovery.org) in their own faith traditions.

FOURTH WEEK OF LENT: WEDNESDAY
Becoming Rooted, Day 45,
"Ancient Contributions"

Forget the events of the past, ignore the things of long ago! Look, I am doing something new! Now it springs forth—can't you see it? I'm making a road in the desert and setting rivers to flow in the wasteland. Wild beasts will honor me—the jackals and the ostriches—for I will put water in the desert and rivers in the wasteland for my chosen people to drink, these people whom I formed for myself so that they might declare my praise.

—Isaiah 43:18–21

People frequently ask me why they have never been taught about
the great Native American civilizations or their contributions
to the world. My answer is always the same: *You weren't supposed
to know.* Our national myths have been designed—on purpose,
with intent—so people never learn these things.

—Randy Woodley, *Becoming Rooted*, 110

Half of my great grandparents came to the United States from the region of Poland, where our prehistoric ancestors built mounds. Several of these earthworks remain and stand as a paragon of Earth-based community art and storytelling across centuries. A few winters ago, I visited the mounds on the edge of the city of Krakow. One of them, Krakus Mound, still serves as a popular tourist destination, the location for an annual spring festival, and is known to have been a significant ritual site for prehistoric Poles. As I spent a few hours alone there on a cold winter morning, I felt more than I was able to process in real-time—respect, curiosity, awe, as well as sadness and loss.

Two of these mounds were built between 200 BCE and 900 CE. Not long after 900 CE, King Mieszko got baptized, known as the "Baptism of Poland," thus history in Poland "officially" began. With it came written language and a new state religion blessed by Rome—a religion that includes over 95 percent of Poles today. Because these mounds predate Christian presence and hegemony in Poland, it makes me wonder about pre-Christian Poland. Poles culturally still practice a few Earth-based spiritual traditions that survived through the centuries, but much like the mounds, the dominant culture dismisses them as prehistoric and irrelevant to the present or future.

Mound Builders lived here in the Americas, too. Incredibly, some of their earthworks remain. Cultures thrived. Consider the city of Cahokia, near present-day St. Louis. Archeologists now compare its peak population to have been the same as or greater than London during the thirteenth century, before its decline less than a century later.

When we honor the Indigenous contributions of the past, it enhances our ability to demonstrate respect for Indigenous peoples now. The colonized mind implicitly undervalues Indigenous contributions to society. Dominant culture has socialized us to normalize the downplaying of historical wrongs against Indigenous peoples.

Lent is a season of remembering, of reconnecting to the Source. Remember the lands you now live on and the First Peoples of those lands. If we respect the contributions of the host peoples of our lands, we will better understand the land itself. When we work together at healing the Earth, we get healed by the Earth together.

Invitation:

Has your municipality joined over one hundred US cities and twelve states to replace Columbus Day with Indigenous People's Day? Which local peoples should be honored? Learn something new about them today and share it.

FOURTH WEEK OF LENT: THURSDAY

Becoming Rooted, Day 46,
"Destruction"

When YHWH, your God, brings you into the land that you are
to enter and take possession of, and drives out multitudes before
you—the Hittites, the Girgashites, the Amorites, the Canaanites,
the Perizzites, the Hivites and the Jebusites, seven nations larger
and stronger than you—and when YHWH, your God, delivers
them to you and you defeat them, you must destroy them entirely.
Make no treaties with them and show them no mercy.

—Deuteronomy 7:1–2

When Indigenous people resisted their own destruction,
subjugation, or the theft of their lands, they were considered
the problem. Those who oppressed them created narratives
that justified their own actions, and these narratives became
myths that inform the worldview of the settler-colonizer.

—Randy Woodley, *Becoming Rooted*, 112

I can barely fathom the scale of destruction endured on Turtle Island (an Indigenous name for North America) since European contact. Whole Indigenous civilizations met with a force that attempted to utterly destroy them without mercy. An expanding dominant culture has been trying to displace and replace the First Peoples from the land ever since. Yet despite historical atrocities and an ongoing White supremacy power dynamic that seeks to destroy them, the Indigenous peoples of this land are still here.

White supremacy culture lies and defends itself to avoid accountability. However, over the past year, I have sensed that more people are listening to the truth about our past. During the summer of 2020, Deb Haaland (Laguna Pueblo), the US Secretary of the Interior, announced the creation of the Federal Indian Boarding School Initiative to review the history and traumatic legacy of the schools.

These government-funded and church-run residential schools' policies, practices, and procedures were to "kill the Indian, save the man." They ran until the 1990s. They were part of a deliberate strategy to undermine legitimate Indigenous rights to the land. These schools and their agents used kidnapping, torture, and other horrifying abuses. Generations of kids endured horrific traumas that were all expressly in the name of Christ. The cultural trauma resulting from these schools touches all Indigenous peoples of this land. Many of the survivors of the residential schools are still alive.

On top of the other traumas endured by survivors, the perpetrators have kept secrets regarding missing or deceased children at the schools. Many of the abusers are still alive. Some difficult secrets of the past will be unearthed through the investigation of unmarked graves at the sites of the boarding schools.

Who will repent and take responsibility when it comes time to return the bodies to their lands, to acknowledge the harm, and attempt to make amends? The government has not yet taken responsibility for its role, nor yet have most faith communities.

Repentance is to turn around. Accountable change in behavior demonstrates inner transformation through both acknowledgment of the impact of the past along with authentic attempts at making amends.

Invitation:

Investigate the National Native American Boarding School Healing Coalition (boardingschoolhealing.org) and see which resources can equip your networks for education and accountability.

FOURTH WEEK OF LENT: FRIDAY

Becoming Rooted, Day 48, "The Trauma and the Cure"

The angel then showed me the river of life-giving water, clear as crystal, which issued from the throne of God and of the Lamb, and flowed down the middle of the streets. On either side of the river grew the trees of life which produce fruit twelve times a year, once each month; their leaves serve as medicine to heal the nations.

—Revelation 22:1–2

A harmonious worldview. Mutual respect. Generosity. Hospitality. Inclusion. Relatedness to all creation. Cooperation. Wisdom. Humor. These are the sureties that we need today to heal ourselves, the Earth, and the whole community of creation.

—Randy Woodley, *Becoming Rooted*, 116

One of my personal benefits of being involved with the work of Eloheh is how Edith and Randy Woodley invite me into a reciprocal relationship with them. It's also an invitation into healing the land and allowing the land to heal us. Perhaps that sounds really abstract, but this process has been and continues to be very tangible for me. I got to visit the new farm in Yamhill, Oregon, with my family a few months ago. We got to visit, help out with some projects, and paint some murals.

This edition of Eloheh Farm is the Woodley family's third foray into manifesting the vision of Eloheh. Back in 2006, the first Eloheh Farm in Kentucky was disturbed by the regular intimidation and hostile acts of their neighboring White ranchers who would not be held in check by local authorities. An emergency relocation proved costly but necessary to protect their children. When I met the Woodleys back in 2012, they lived on a small farm of fewer than four acres in Oregon, near the seminary at which Randy taught and I studied. Despite its diminutive size relative to their first farm, and despite being surrounded on three sides by conventionally grown hazelnuts treated with pesticides that affected the plants and animals, Eloheh lived on. The farm offered a physical place and a holistic teaching and cultural center both for Natives and non-Natives.

Then in 2019, Erna Kim Hackett, another former student of Randy's, and I responded to Randy and Edith's invitation to tell the truth about wrongs they endured and give people today a chance to do something right about it. The communities responded by raising over $100,000 through #ResurrectEloheh—funds which proved critical in their ability to purchase nearly ten acres only a few miles away.

Visiting Eloheh Farm in person made me feel how real some miracles are. So many peoples' labor has gone into the process so far. Our multi-year campaign did not reach an end but became a new beginning of the journey, one full of humor, respect, generosity, and relatedness. As I was leaving, I caught a glimpse of returning camas plants growing wild. The land itself, it seemed, was smiling back at me.

Invitation:

Connect with Eloheh Indigenous Center for Earth Justice (eloheh.org/the-center-for-earth-justice) today by following on social media or signing up for the email list. Discern how you're able to get involved—whether buying some seeds, volunteering on the farm, being part of an upcoming learning session, or just making a donation.

FOURTH WEEK OF LENT: SATURDAY

Becoming Rooted, Day 50,
"Unreconciled Knowledge"

My sisters and brothers, what good is it to profess faith without practicing it? Such faith has no power to save. If any are in need of clothes and have no food to live on, and one of you says to them, "Goodbye and good luck. Stay warm and well-fed," without giving them the bare necessities of life, then what good is this? So it is with faith. If good deeds don't go with it, faith is dead.

—James 2:14–17

What will we do with the knowledge we gain? How does knowing about injustice change us? How does it change the stories we tell about ourselves and our nation?

—Randy Woodley, *Becoming Rooted*, 121

The Western worldview that formed me elevates beliefs above behaviors, intentions above impact, and faith above works. This dualistic mentality allows us to understand our spirits as separate from our bodies, the future as separate from the past, and our behaviors as not necessarily reflective of our beliefs. In an individualistic culture, our deepest sense of being is how we see ourselves as separate individuals.

Our moment in time calls us to embrace a more holistic and connected worldview. The past calls us to break paternalistic patterns of relating and dysfunctional power dynamics. We need to listen to the truth about the past and act differently based on what we learn. We need to recover our interrelatedness with creation in order for future generations of humans to live on Earth. What happens during this historical moment will be remembered by future generations. The future will measure us according to our ability to change and enact changes.

During Lent, we remember that moving through darkness to light is possible. Jesus didn't choose the path that led to his own comfort; he walked into his calling. To become rooted more deeply in creation and Creator is to live into this community of creation, which is full of support and full of examples and demonstrations for how to go deeper. Today it's just about taking your next step.

FIFTH WEEK OF LENT: SUNDAY

Becoming Rooted, Day 56, "Individualism"

After John's arrest, Jesus appeared in Galilee proclaiming the Good News of God: "This is the time of fulfillment. The reign of God is at hand! Change your hearts and minds, and believe this Good News!"

—Mark 1:14–15

One of the traits Western humans seem to have laid aside somewhere is cooperation for the good of the group— the common good, as some call it....We might be the most individualistic society in the history of the world.

—Randy Woodley, *Becoming Rooted*, 135–136

April 4th is the anniversary of the assassination of Rev. Dr. Martin Luther King, Jr. During his short life, Dr. King was arrested nineteen times—the same number of trips that Harriet Tubman made back to the South to free enslaved people after she escaped North. After one of his arrests, while he sat in a Birmingham jail cell, King wrote a long letter to White pastors on the margins of a newspaper and smuggled it out to get it published.

In his letter from a Birmingham jail, Dr. King articulated a profound spiritual conviction that is both biblical and non-Western. In that cell, Dr. King let out the secret to love and liberation:

> It really boils down to this: that all life is interrelated. We are all caught in an inescapable network of mutuality, tied together into a single garment of destiny. Whatever affects one directly, affects all indirectly.

Dr. King's letter challenged White pastors and their congregations to repent. In the writings of the ancient historian Josephus, repentance (Greek *metanoia)* described someone changing sides during a time of war. Someone who repented was a traitor!

Dr. King challenged White Christians to break rank with a Western "progress" obsessed with personal piety and individual rights—a "progress" that came at the expense of the common good. When King reminded White folks and middle-class people that they were caught in an inescapable network of mutuality, he was not only recruiting them to join the Black freedom struggle but also beckoning them to break rank with a worldview that made them more defensive, depressed, lonely, anxious, controlling, competitive, oblivious and entitled. King was offering folks what we all need to heal and recover. What Randy Woodley calls "the harmony way."

We break rank with the Western worldview so that we can *become* something different—so that our lives will be illuminated by intimacy, vulnerability, presence, playfulness, tenderness, trust, mutuality, mystery, wonder, awe, accountability, awareness, appreciation, curiosity, compassion, confidence, humility, open-heartedness and emotional expressiveness. As Black southern writer Imani Perry wrote to White people in the wake of George Floyd's murder, "If you join us, you might feel not only our pain but also the beauty of being human."

Invitation:

Invite a kindred to have a conversation about what you might break rank with in order to live congruently with the inescapable network of mutuality.

FIFTH WEEK OF LENT: MONDAY

Becoming Rooted, Day 60,
"Earth Rights"

And people never put new wine in an old wineskin. If they do, the new wine will burst the skin; the wine will spill out and the skin will be ruined.

—Luke 5:37

Only a worldview embracing the whole community of creation will sustain the quality of life we all want to enjoy.

—Randy Woodley, *Becoming Rooted*, 144

According to author and activist Nick Estes,* a citizen of the Lower Brule Sioux Tribe, the Indigenous way to resist Western progress is to keep asking what proliferates in the absence of Empire. As summarized in the title of Estes's book *Our History is the Future*, we must go back to the spirituality of our deep ancestors that thrived for thousands of years.

This ancient-future faith is scripted on the first few pages of the Bible, right after the humans get booted from the garden. That's when Abel shows up, still living sustainably on the land as a *tender of sheep*. His brother Cain is *a tiller of soil*. Abel's sacrifice found divine favor because it flowed from an Indigenous pastoral nomadic lifestyle of trust—in contrast to the civilized methods of Cain, built on conquest and control. Abel and Cain represent a contest of lifeways. They had completely different orientations to land and different relationships to labor.**

In the Bible, Abel represents those who are consistently disappeared by "settlers" who, like Cain, understand progress as taking property and flipping it for a profit. Abel was a shepherd, those known as the first social and political resisters in history. Shepherds exited populated cities with their flocks, living on wilderness land beyond the reach of their imperial bosses. The shed blood of shepherd Abel cries out to God. Cain is spared, but he is consigned to a wandering existence. Cain became a "settler," trampling other people's land wherever he wandered. Sure, the people east of Eden didn't kill him. But they didn't trust him either.

The way forward is by fermenting new wine from the old ways of Indigenous peoples and the prophetic strand of Scripture—starting with Abel, living sustainably on the land, and kept alive by Miriam, Moses, Jonah, Jeremiah, John the buck-wild baptizer, and Jesus of Nazareth. This sacred lifestyle cannot be contained in the old institutional wineskins of Western civilization. We must create new wineskins that are non-hierarchical, cooperative, collaborative, and committed to sustainable practices that subvert the so-called "progress" percolating with supremacy, certainty, and celebrity.

* See Nick Estes's *Our History is the Future* (2019).

** See James Perkinson's *Messianism Against Christology* (2013).

Invitation:

What would it look like for the new wine of "the harmony way" to fill up new wineskins of worship, of family, of education, of banking, of shopping, of eating, of housing, of playing, of partying, of parenting?

FIFTH WEEK OF LENT: TUESDAY

Becoming Rooted, Day 57,
"To Be Human On Earth"

Jesus saw the heavens opening and the Spirit descending on
him like a dove. Then a voice came from the heavens: "You
are my Beloved, my Own. On you my favor rests."

—Mark 1:10b–11

One reason Indigenous peoples have been condemned is
because we view our relationship with the Earth as very
sacred. Indigenous peoples understand our relationship with
creation as necessary in order to experience the abundant
life Great Spirit intends for us and for all humanity.

—Randy Woodley, *Becoming Rooted*, 137–138

To help me hear the heavenly voice and live the harmony way, I am harkening back to Pelagius, a Welsh monk who was declared a heretic in the fifth century by St. Augustine, St. Jerome, the Pope, and Western Christianity ever since. Pelagius had the audacity to believe that human beings are inherently beautiful and beloved.

Pelagius had an Indigenous advantage. He came from the people known by ancient Greeks and Romans as *keltoi*—the Celtic people—the "strangers" or "hidden ones" living on the northwestern fringes of Empire (eventually Ireland, England, Scotland, Wales). The Celts were village people before they were colonized by Roman Christians. They emphasized intimate relationship over rational knowledge. They practiced an Earth spirituality of hospitality and blessing.

The Celts believed in a creative and nurturing Force that flowed through everything, including ourselves. The divinity they called Danu was a feminine force, weaving the world together through wonder and love. The Celts celebrated each other and the Earth. When they converted to Christianity, the Celts—in ways very similar to the Black church in North America—synthesized their Indigenous convictions with the way of Jesus. One of their most cherished saints sang of citizens of heaven drinking in a lake of beer together for all eternity!

Unfortunately, the Celtic brand of Christianity has been sidelined by an imperial brand of Christianity that pressed cancel on Pelagius. Celtic peoples became colonized by empires that demanded their allegiance and identity in the pursuit of "progress." Indigenous nuances were erased as racial categories created a caste system. My ancestors, who came to North America, became White. They were spiritually hoodwinked by the hierarchy of the Western worldview.

Whiteness, according to theologian Dr. Willie Jennings,* is not a term that refers to people of European descent, but instead to a way of being in the world and seeing in the world that distorts the Indigenous emphasis on community and intimacy. Whiteness pursues a kind of "progress" that strangles the notion that we are intimately connected to God, ancestors, and every living being. The ancient heretic Pelagius can help us reclaim the same universal bond of biblical belovedness that birthed the Jesus movement: the Indigenous belief that we *belong* to everything that exists.

* See Willie Jennings's *After Whiteness: An Education in Belonging* (2020).

Invitation:

Before you do anything else, make Pelagius proud and resist "progress." For a few minutes, breathe in your inherent divine belovedness.

FIFTH WEEK OF LENT: WEDNESDAY

Becoming Rooted, Day 53, "Deconstructing Worldview"

What comparison can I make with this generation? They are like children shouting to others as they sit in the marketplace, "We piped you a tune, but you wouldn't dance. We sang you a dirge, but you wouldn't mourn."

—Matthew 11:16–17

Part of the problem with a Western worldview is that we spend too much time in our own heads, thinking and rethinking, but not enough time acting on our thoughts. To change, we need to embody our thoughts in the world.

—Randy Woodley, *Becoming Rooted*, 129–130

Two weeks after George Floyd was murdered, Dr. James Perkinson preached to a predominantly White church in Detroit about de-centering Whiteness in ourselves and the world around us. He challenged us to become smaller by reducing our footprint on the planet and the space we take up in social gatherings. This requires urgency, intentionality, and large doses of humility. However, Perkinson also prodded us to get bigger emotionally and spiritually—to develop what he calls "a muscular inner capacity" that can "express big feelings, without embodying grandiosity or dissolving into guilt and shame and fear."

The Black, lesbian, mother, warrior, and poet Audre Lorde called this muscular inner capacity "the erotic." In a legendary essay* from the late 1970s, she animated the erotic as "a non-european consciousness," a non-rational, spiritual, and feminine plane, which has been suppressed by White male models of power. Lorde wrote that men keep women around to benefit from this power but that they fear it too much to examine and tap into the erotic within themselves.

The erotic subverts the stoicism and self-sufficiency of the Western worldview by sharing passion and pursuits and building bridges and bonds that lessen the threat of difference. The erotic opens up the capacity for joy in every mundane or dutiful thing we do. Unlike the meditating ascetic, the erotic embraces emotion, refusing self-negation and numbness. It is about being conscious of what we are feeling at any given moment and sharing it with someone else. In short, the erotic cultivates embodiment and belongingness.

The erotic is both indigenous and biblical. Jesus lamented his own generation, struggling to tap into celebration and sorrow. They simply could not move with the music played by the children of the marketplace. Jesus modeled the erotic through main characters like the Good Samaritan and the Running Father, who are not pouting, passive-aggressive, distancing, abusive, controlling, manipulative, cynical, indifferent, above the fray, apathetic, objective, or neutral. They are driven by compassion (Greek *splagchna*), literally a bowel-bursting, gut-busting solidarity with those who suffer. Their feeling leads them to take risks by taking sides. They pursue what is right, which we can never do if what is right is imprisoned in our heads.

* See Audre Lorde's "Uses of the Erotic: The Erotic as Power" (1978).

Invitation:

Practice getting smaller and getting bigger at the same time. Reduce your footprint on the planet and your size in social spaces. But also let the erotic expand your soul.

FIFTH WEEK OF LENT: THURSDAY

Becoming Rooted, Day 51,
"Generosity"

I was a stranger [immigrant] and you welcomed me...

—Matthew 25:35b

The truth is, every time you did this for the least of
my sisters or brothers, you did it for me.

—Matthew 25:40b

Indigenous people have been able to thrive in what seem the most
inhospitable climates and geographies imaginable.... Yet despite these
hardships, Indigenous people in North America have developed values
based on generosity, hospitality, and concern for the common good.

—Randy Woodley, *Becoming Rooted*, 125–126

"We who are dark," W.E.B. Du Bois once wrote, "can see America in ways that White Americans cannot." This spiritual reality is the basis for my own Lenten journey and for my own life conversion. Back in 2003, I met a young man speaking in broken English who had just missed the bus to get to his job. On our drive together down the freeway, he told me that he was from Honduras. I asked how he got to California. He walked. More than three thousand miles. He had to leave his home country because American corporations were pursuing "progress" there by stealing land for "resources."

In this same season of life, I was leading short-term Evangelical mission trips to Mexico and Africa and inner-city America. While I was certain that I was doing all these folks a favor, they were rearranging the relationship. They were reversing my mission trips! In their faces, I found the risen Jesus evangelizing me into a way that subverted my Western worldview. Jesus was teaching me a different brand of greatness through the lives of those that society calls "the least." Just like he said he would.

A decade later, I learned about Berta Cáceres, a Honduran community organizer who was assassinated in her own home two days before her forty-fifth birthday. She had been on the military hit list for years because she led her Indigenous community—the Lenca—in a nonviolent rebellion against the mining and dam projects of corporate developers with deep ties to American investors.

Berta committed her life to conspiring for the Lenca people, who believe that they come from the Earth, water, and corn and are called to be guardians of the rivers that sustain every form of life. In this daring vocation, they believe that they are protected and guided by the spirits of young girls who teach them how to give their lives for the well-being of humanity and the planet.

Berta boldly broke rank from a "progress" perpetuated by the profit motive, building a world that works for Black, Indigenous, and Immigrant communities, women, queer folk, and for Mother Earth and her more-than-human creatures. Berta knew that the harmony way will never die. It rises up and walks thousands of miles to beckon us to break rank with what is killing the planet—and our souls.

Invitation:

Tweak what you are reading and watching. Get scripted by authors and directors who are dark. They can see America—and Spirit—in ways that White Americans cannot.

FIFTH WEEK OF LENT: FRIDAY

Becoming Rooted, Day 58, "Plastic Spirit"

In the fifteenth year of the reign of Emperor Tiberius, when Pontius Pilate was governor of Judea, and Herod was ruler of Galilee, and his brother Philip ruler of the region of Ituraea and Trachonitis, and Lysanias ruler of Abilene, during the high priesthood of Annas and Caiaphas, the word of God came to John son of Zechariah in the wilderness.

—Luke 3:1–2, NRSV

…I attended a Native American men's retreat in the land of the Nooksack people. The more familiar way to describe its location is to say that it was near the border of Washington state and British Columbia…. a mythical nationstate border, however, [that] centers both George Washington and Christopher Columbus.

—Randy Woodley, *Becoming Rooted*, 139

Just ten miles south from where I grew up in Southern California's San Juan Creek watershed is a freeway off-ramp called Cristianitos. Spanish for "little Christians." The road starts a stone's throw from Richard Nixon's Western White House overlooking the Pacific Ocean and heads east to the entrance of the Camp Pendleton Marine Base, very close to the site of the very first baptism in California history in 1769. Two young girls from the Acjachemen tribe were deathly ill, and the company of soldiers and priests crusading through the region could not heal them. So they converted them into little Christians so that they could go to heaven when they would soon die.

Local Indigenous author and activist Dina Gilio-Whitaker* taught me that Cristianitos Road runs right through the sacred land of Panhe, an Acjachemen burial and ceremonial site at the coastal border of Orange and San Diego counties. The Acjachemen people are not recognized by the federal government—despite archeological proof that they lived sustainably on that land for more than 9,000 years before European Christians invaded it and stole it and forcibly converted them to the cult of Jesus, the White conquistador.

To add insult to injury, the European Christians raped their women and infected them with their diseases. Panhe was the epicenter of a genocidal cocktail of disease centuries before the novel coronavirus came for a country trying to make itself great again in every colonial way possible. The people of Panhe were victims of a COVID-19 on steroids. As more than 90 percent of the Indigenous population of Turtle Island was killed off, White Christians spurned social distancing for what they called "progress."

Panhe is the crucified wound of a people still surviving but totally unrecognized. In fact, its sacred quality is soaked in the surreal statistic that 99.999 percent of those who call California home drive by Panhe thousands of times and never even know it exists. Ancient Oak and Sycamore trees of Panhe remember a time when White people were not around. They are *still* standing despite the encroachment of a military base, major freeway, nuclear power plant, state campground, and Trestles, one of the most legendary surf beaches in the world. Panhe is a reminder that while politicians are front-page news, the word of God speaks from the wilderness.

* See Dina Gilio-Whitaker's *As Long As The Grass Grows: The Indigenous Fight for Environmental Justice, From Colonization to Standing Rock* (2019).

Invitation:

Find out what your context was called by the people who tended it sustainably for thousands of years. Call it that for the rest of your life—as a reminder to live like they did.

FIFTH WEEK OF LENT: SATURDAY

Becoming Rooted, Day 52, "Whole Reality"

Consider the ravens: they neither sow nor reap, they have
neither storehouse nor barn, and yet God feeds them.

—Luke 12:24a, NRSV

What if we understood the Earth itself as our primary spiritual
teacher? Then nothing would be without spirit in our understanding.
Everything would be understood as related. All life would be sacred.
If this were the case, might we be living in a different world today?

—Randy Woodley, *Becoming Rooted*, 128

Consider the dragonfly, who showed up while we were floating on a mountain lake, a few steps off the Pacific Crest Trail. For most of her life, this exquisite Being is just an aquatic nymph without wings. She lives just below the surface of the water. She breathes out of the gills in her rectum. She reminded me that Western "progress" stays on the surface, pursuing legacy projects and building brands. Our ego games make about as much sense as breathing out of our butts. Like Spirit Herself, the dragonfly hovers over the waters. She beckons me to lighten up like her. To stop taking myself so seriously. So I, too, can fly.

Consider the hummingbird, fluttering two feet from my face. She stayed for seven seconds. Seemed like a minute. I didn't mind that she wasn't socially distancing. She pivoted and perched on the tomato trellis—then returned to get in my grill again. This messenger of the divine was delivering joy. She's an expert in ecstasy. She travels thousands of miles a year searching for sweetness. She beckoned me to savor the small stuff and to release the toxins weighing me down. How did she know that, for decades, I've chosen duty over delight?

Consider the bats, nocturnal Beings who came out of their roosts while we sat around the fire swapping stories. Bats energize the local ecology, pollinating and dispersing seeds. Bats also provide pest control. Their diets consist largely of insects like mosquitos, beetles, and termites. Bats do little things that make big things happen. Even their feces has a special name. Guano. Farmers pay top dollar for its fertilizing capacities. That night, the bats were calling me to contribute to the community of creation without being noticed. To be ecological, not egological.

Consider the ravens, they spurn the storehouse and the barn because they do not believe in "progress." Consider the five sparrows sold for two coins, yet God does not forget them. Consider the Great Spirit on the first page of the Scriptures, hovering in the dark over the depths. Hovering. The same Hebrew word is used in Deuteronomy for a mother eagle hovering over her nest. Divine Spirit is a mother bird in motion, methodically and mysteriously sustaining Her young. She does not calculate and control from a throne. She hovers over the deep and dark places of our lives.

Invitation:

Consider the winged Beings wherever you go. What are they trying to teach you?

SIXTH WEEK OF LENT: SUNDAY

Becoming Rooted, Day 61, "Harmony Way"

When you enter the land I am giving you, the land itself must
observe a Sabbath for YHWH. For six years you may sow your
fields and prune your vineyards and gather their crops. But in the
seventh year the land is to have a Sabbath of rest, a Sabbath for
YHWH. Do not sow your fields and do not prune your vineyards.
Do not harvest what grows of itself, or store the grapes of your
untended vines. It will be a year of complete rest for the land.

—Leviticus 25:2b–5

Our Cherokee people have a construct—a way of being—we call *Eloheh*.
This lifeway includes our history, culture, law, and all aspects of life....
[I]t means "the harmony way," but it is so much more.... Eloheh is
knowing the importance of community above oneself and your role in it.

—Randy Woodley, *Becoming Rooted*, 149

Take a moment and imagine your community taking a full year of Sabbath every seventh year, a year of rest for the land, people, and animals, as God instructs in today's passage from Leviticus 25. Can you imagine this happening in the United States?

This sabbatical year is just one piece of the vision God had for the Israelites as they were liberated from slavery in Egypt. This vision was for *shalom*, a Hebrew word that means holistic peace and well-being. The Israelites recently escaped enslavement, and they dreamed and listened to God about a society where they would be safe; no one would have to experience what they had been through. They received this vision of a rhythm of sabbath: rests every seventh day, every seventh year a sabbatical for the land, livestock, and wild animals, and every seven-times-seventh year a year of jubilee, all debts forgiven and each person returns to their family's land (Lev. 25:8–55). The law contained other instructions ensuring everyone would have what they needed, such as leaving the edges of the fields available for gleaners and animals and a range of laws protecting widows, orphans, and immigrants. This *shalom* community was in balance with the land and other creatures, ensuring the community thrived through equitable access to land and had the opportunity for regular rest. Jesus came not to abolish this law but to remind us of the wisdom behind it, leading to equity, healing, and right relationships with God and others.

The Hebrew word *shalom* has a similar meaning to the Cherokee word *Eloheh*. This is a concept known in many Indigenous cultures, but I can't think of a word in English that can convey that meaning. In a community practicing *shalom* or *Eloheh*, we recognize we are participants nestled within a group, supported by and supporting the whole.

I find it difficult to take a regular sabbath, let alone a sabbatical year, because of the United States' ultimate value of productivity. Practicing a sabbath is intensely counter-cultural: it requires us to defy our culture's label of what gives value, instead living into our worth as human beings, created in the image of God, participating in the community of all life. *Eloheh* and *shalom* can be called the harmony way: being ourselves within the healthy rhythms of rest and of care for people, God, and land.

Invitation:

If you can, take a sabbath today. It may not be possible to take the whole day of rest without some planning, but you could perhaps set aside a segment of your day. Additionally, plan for next sabbath, either Saturday or Sunday, or whichever day works with your schedule.

SIXTH WEEK OF LENT: MONDAY

Becoming Rooted, Day 62,
"Like Water on a Windshield"

Woe to those who plot trouble, who lie in bed planning evil! When morning comes they carry it out, because they're the ones in power. They see a field and they seize it, a house, and they take it over. They defraud people of their homes, then extort them of their land as well.

—Micah 2:1–2

We truly believe we are much smarter than the generations and civilizations that came before us. Yet none of those prior generations destroyed the very Earth that feeds them and maintains their existence as a species.

—Randy Woodley, Becoming Rooted, 152

My great-grandmother, Fannie Beebe (1900–1985), raised five children during the Depression. She canned garden produce for winter in a homestead without electricity. A woman of strong faith, she taught Sunday school and donated land for a Quaker meetinghouse.

Granny Fannie, as my mom's generation called her, had vast knowledge of how to live off the grid that has not been passed down; much has been lost in three generations. My mom remembers Granny slaughtering a chicken with an ax, bringing it in for Sunday supper. Fannie wrote in a letter in 1914: "It is now 7:20 a.m. and I have made up two beds and straightened up the bedroom and front room and sitting room and living room, piled one pile of sage brush [sic] and burnt two piles, now I'm ready to write. Haven't much to tell. Tuesday evening after supper I went out with the gun and was out about 15 minutes and shot three rabbits…."

She and my great-grandpa, Glen, were the first European Americans to settle 420 acres in eastern Oregon, not conducive to settlement until the Owyhee Dam facilitated irrigation. Seen as a major sign of progress at the time, the dam created farmland from the desert. Granny called their lives a "bargain with God": they put in hard work, and God "blessed" them with the land. But farming this region also required destruction of the delicate high desert ecosystem, tearing out sagebrush, and tilling the soil.

Additionally, the land was never ceded by the Cayuse, Shoshone, or Paiute tribes forcibly removed from the region. These tribes managed the land for centuries (if not millennia), learning what the land needed, what could be used, and how to care for it. Tribal spokespeople stated they could not sell their land. The God who had given them the land had created the Earth and made them of it: it was not theirs to sell. Removing them from the land was like removing an infant from its mother's breast.

My great-grandparents were hard-working Christians, doing their best to eke out a living on a difficult landscape. They also lived in a way critiqued in Micah 2:1–2, benefiting from building dams "because it is in their power," coveting and seizing the fields of Indigenous people, and claiming the land as their children's inheritance. Is this progress? Should we participate in "progress" if it requires ecosystem destruction and oppression?

Invitation:

Consider things your ancestors knew how to do, but you do not know. Is there a skill or practice you would like to recover? What is it? Make a concrete plan for how and when you will begin learning that skill or practice.

SIXTH WEEK OF LENT: TUESDAY

Becoming Rooted, Day 63,
"Seeds"

Listen carefully. Imagine a sower going out to sow, scattering the seed widely. Some of the seed fell on the edge of the path, and the birds came and ate it. Some seed fell on rocky ground where it found a little soil, and sprang up immediately because the soil had little depth—but then, when the sun came up and scorched it, it withered for lack of roots. Some seed fell into thorns, and the thorns grew up and choked it, and it produced no crop. And some seed fell into rich soil and grew tall and strong, producing a crop thirty, sixty, even a hundredfold.

—Mark 4:3–8

Edith and I have had hundreds and perhaps thousands of people visit us…Our time with visitors usually begins with a farm tour.…
On one of those farm tours, I heard Edith use a phrase that resonated deeply with me. She said, "I believe in the seeds."

—Randy Woodley, *Becoming Rooted*, 154

"I didn't realize a pea is a seed!" a college student exclaimed one day as we were working in a campus community garden. With a huge smile of wonder and anticipation, they received a handful of wrinkly dry peas into their palm and placed each one carefully into the shallow furrow, covering them carefully with soil with their fingertips as I showed them. With minimal intervention from us besides patience and a little structure, the sun, soil, and rain did their work, and the pea seeds grew into a mess of vines, pea pods dangling, each small pea from the previous year becoming hundreds or thousands more peas.

This reminds me of the parable of the sower. The farmer in the story shares the seeds freely, even feeding the birds, trusting the land to receive and grow the seeds, trusting the seeds to flourish in the places they could. This parable expresses an attitude of abundance, trust, and sharing: the farmer believes in the seeds.

When I learned the parable of the sower as a child, I learned it as a warning, a cautionary tale, that I need to strive to be good, to be worthy of the seed of the good news, to fear that maybe my seed will be snatched away or will wither. This interpretation comes from a fear of scarcity and an interpretation that each individual is alone as we attempt to grasp and grow a single precious seed.

But what if we have simply forgotten what seeds look like? What if, like my student, we can learn to recognize the seeds all around us, nourishing us today, and capable of becoming an abundant crop if only we plant them? What if we see the farmer in this parable sowing seeds with joy and abundance, trusting that the wild creatures will receive nourishment and that there will be an overflowing crop as the sun, water, and soil do their work? What if we participate in this work of the entire community of creation? What if we also believe in the seeds?

Invitation:

Plant something and/or make a garden plan for this season. Maybe you plant a flower or herb in a pot in your window, or maybe you have an outdoor area where you could plant. Consider joining a community garden. Attend to the metaphorical and physical seeds around you, practicing trust in abundance.

SIXTH WEEK OF LENT: WEDNESDAY

Becoming Rooted, Day 66,
"The Joy of Wild-Tending"

God gave Solomon very great wisdom, discernment, and breadth of understanding as vast as the sand on the seashore.... He would speak of trees, from the cedar that is in the Lebanon to the hyssop that grows in the wall; he would speak of animals, and birds, and reptiles, and fish. People came from all the nations to hear the wisdom of Solomon; they came from all the kings of the earth who had heard of his wisdom.

—1 Kings 4:29, 33–34, NRSV

The Indigenous people of the land are the original wild-tenders. Everything from deer to plants to the use of water was carefully kept in balance so there would be enough left to sustain them in the future and for generations to come.

—Randy Woodley, *Becoming Rooted*, 160–161

When I was about four, my dad had my sister and me pick dandelion leaves for a stew. It tasted disgusting, and the story became legend in our family—I didn't know anyone else who had eaten dandelions! And yet, I remembered. As an adult, I have picked dandelions with my children to make stew, fried blossoms, and dandelion cookies. As a preschooler, my son delightedly collected dandelions on our walks, excited to participate in gathering food for our family. We had to discuss which plants were likely safe and which ones may have been sprayed with chemicals. The same goes for blackberries. Both species are invasive but better put to good use than not. My kids and I also delight in discovering patches of huckleberries, salal berries, thimbleberries, miner's lettuce, wood sorrel, and chanterelle mushroom when we are out on hikes.

The Bible praises the wisdom of Solomon, including his knowledge and awareness of the plants and animals in his region. I usually think of him sitting on a throne, arbitrating or receiving foreign dignitaries, but this passage from 1 Kings tells us he knew about trees, hyssop, and a range of animals. Now I picture Solomon ranging around the countryside, learning about and from the creatures around him. Hyssop is a shrub with medicinal properties. I wonder what he noticed as he wild-tended the land under his care and how time in the community of creation informed his suggestions to people in conflict or with illnesses. It seems that Solomon became distracted later in life, letting himself be drawn away by wealth and excessive pleasures. I wonder what would have happened if he had spent time in the wilderness with his children, teaching them what he knew, and building up their wisdom in the lifeways of the land.

In our own time, much wisdom has been lost on Turtle Island: forcibly removed with Indigenous people displaced to other landscapes, slowly choked with the requirement of children in Indian boarding schools to not speak their native languages, and crowded out with invasive species, human infrastructure, and pollutants in soil and water. In line with the wisdom of Solomon and the work of reconciliation that is supposed to define Christian faith, it is time to return to seeking wild-tended wisdom, listening with humility to other species in our regions and the people who can introduce us to them.

Invitation:

Consider what wild foods you know of that grow in your region. If you already know some that are in season, pick some and eat them as a reminder of the life-giving sustenance that is all around us in God's overflowing grace and bounty. If you don't know of any, find a person or a book you can learn from.

SIXTH WEEK OF LENT: THURSDAY
Becoming Rooted, Day 67, "Tolerance"

Citizens of Athens, I note that in every respect you are scrupulously religious. As I walked about looking at your shrines, I even discovered an altar inscribed, "To an Unknown God."…For the God who made the world and all that is in it…doesn't live in sanctuaries made by human hands.…From one person God created all of humankind to inhabit the entire earth, and set…the exact place where each nation should dwell. God did this so that human beings would seek, reach out for, and perhaps find the One who is not really far from any of us.

—Acts 17:22b–23a, 24, 26–27

[S]ince the days of Greece and Rome, the West has seen itself as the highest form of civilization on Earth. Members of Western civilization have so normalized and universalized that understanding…that societies that don't share those same principles are seen as suspect, if not primitive or savage.

—Randy Woodley, *Becoming Rooted*, 162

In today's passage from Acts, Paul connects with the Greek and Roman citizens of Athens by pointing out one of their gods to whom he could relate. He found a truth in their religion and reached out to their common humanity, their common groping after God, even when God can seem mysterious. And yet, Paul says, God is not far from any of us. According to Paul, God is already at work: people are searching for and finding God.

This is perhaps a challenging teaching for many Christians because we think of our way as the only way, the superior way, the way others must follow. While it is central to our tradition to share the good news about Jesus' message and resurrection, those of us from Western Christianity tend to also want to share our culture, values, and social structure as a necessary part of the gospel, an idea not well-grounded in Scripture. Jesus' earliest followers realized they needed to strip cultural expectations and focus on love.

Eventually, the culture Paul reached out to—passed down through the empires of Athens and Rome—took on this strange religion of hope for the underdog and used it as justification for conquest. Under the guise of spreading Jesus' message of good news for the poor, European empires coerced and stole, caused violence to people and land, destroyed ecosystems, and considered other cultures uncivilized.

What if European Christians had taken Paul's example, and instead of conquering and destroying, had looked for points of connection? What if the ancestors of European Americans had the humility of the early Jewish followers of Jesus, who realized their cultural practices were not the point, but the value they found in other human beings, and the connection they shared when they found others who were also reaching for and finding the "unknown god"?

In our own time, may we make a better choice. We know God is present with those who are marginalized for unjust reasons, and we know God is at work in communities expressing hope and care, sharing with those who are in need. May we seek out the ways God is at work—and join in.

Invitation:

Consider the difference between tolerating someone whose beliefs and cultural practices differ from yours and resisting unjust treatment of others. Are there ways you're being invited to build tolerance by seeking out the humanity of those around you? Are there ways you're being nudged to stand in courageous solidarity with those who are being harmed?

SIXTH WEEK OF LENT: FRIDAY

Becoming Rooted, Day 68,
"Respect for Elders"

My children, learn from my wisdom, and concentrate on what words I say;
don't let them get out of your sight, but keep them deep in your heart.
They'll give you life if you live by them; they're good for your body and
soul. Most of all, watch over your heart, because it's the wellspring of life.

—Proverbs 4:20–23

One of the most difficult things for outsiders to do when entering Indian
country is to listen....If an elder takes the time to lend their wisdom to a
situation, we listen without interruption—no matter how long they talk.

—Randy Woodley, *Becoming Rooted*, 164

In June of 2021, I had the opportunity to attend the Treaty People Gathering in Minnesota at the request of Anishinaabe elders. They invited people to take action to demand President Biden stop the Line 3 pipeline. Along with thousands of other people—including an interfaith delegation of four hundred—we spent several days learning about the region and the practices of the Anishinaabe women who are the tribe's water protectors, growing in our awareness of the legal and environmental concerns surrounding Line 3.

The pipeline (switched on in October of 2021) traverses land where the Anishinaabe hold treaty rights and crosses over two hundred waterways. It transports Canadian tar sands, one of the dirtiest fossil fuels, and if allowed to continue for its full lifespan, will facilitate greenhouse gas emissions equivalent to fifty coal-fired power plants. Pipeline construction has already caused chemical spills, damage to aquifers, and habitat destruction.

After fighting the pipeline's construction in all possible legal avenues as the project made its way through environmental impact studies and permitting processes, the Anishinaabe hosted the Treaty People Gathering to engage in mass civil disobedience, to disobey unjust laws to draw attention to the harm done by fossil fuel companies, governmental bodies, police officers, and each of us who use fossil fuels. One day in early June, hundreds of activists were arrested at one location for trespassing, and hundreds of others of us gathered on a boardwalk in the beautiful marshes near the Mississippi headwaters, praying together for the future of our common home.

The Anishinaabe women elders reminded us we are all "treaty people" if we live on this land called Turtle Island or the United States. Treaties between the Anishinaabe and the American government include rights to hunt, fish, perform rituals, and harvest wild rice that grows only in those wetlands. For those of us of European descent, are we willing to uphold our ancestors' word? Do we have the integrity to at the very least follow the treaties?

The elders leading this part of the movement for climate justice have a quiet, fierce, wise, and deep strength that gives me hope and courage. They invited us in, even though many of us descend from those who stole their land, and they extend again and again a hand of friendship and collaboration. May we all learn to be this kind of elder in our own fullness of years, and until then, may we listen and follow.

Invitation:

Find out what treaties were signed with Indigenous peoples where you live. Are these being followed today? If not, what is one thing you will do to work toward the integrity of living up to our collective promises?

SIXTH WEEK OF LENT: SATURDAY

Becoming Rooted, Day 69,
"Solving Modern Problems"

Some…said, "Why do your disciples violate the tradition of the elders?"…
Jesus replied, "And why do you violate the commandments of God for
the sake of your tradition? For God said, 'Honor your mother and your
father'…But you say, 'Whoever says to their parents, "Any support you
might have had from me is dedicated to God," is no longer obligated
to support them.'…Isaiah prophesied well when he said of you: 'These
people honor me with their lips, while their hearts are far from me. Their
worship of me is worthless, and their doctrines are mere human rules.'"

—Matthew 15:1–9 (selections)

We live in a crazy, fast-paced, technological world. Too much technology
has been and continues to be developed without concern for the
community of creation. Shouldn't we listen to the wisdom of the
people who have lived on the land for tens of thousands of years?

—Randy Woodley, *Becoming Rooted*, 167

Lent traditionally includes a time of fasting, placing our focus on God. Perhaps we give up something we enjoy so we can remember to attend to God whenever we have a hankering for a sweet treat or stimulating cup of caffeine. These can be meaningful reminders.

It's also important to not only do this action just because it's a "tradition of the elders." Jesus pointed out that although the religious leaders may follow a surface-level ritual, they fail to follow a more important commandment, instead finding ways to evade their responsibility through creative sidestepping of the intention behind the law. He said the religious leaders say all the right words, but their hearts are not seeking after God. Imagine being those to whom he is speaking, who have devoted their lives and sacrificed much in the way of personal comfort to follow the letter of the law as they understood it—and he has the gall to call them hypocrites?

What might Jesus say to us about our own fasting practices during Lent, particularly if we are people with economic and social privileges? Maybe something like this? "You gave up chocolate for forty days, but your money is invested in industries that spew toxic gasses into the air, causing asthma and lung disease in the 'least of these' and destroying this planet's ability to comfortably sustain life for generations into the future."

These are challenging words to hear for those of us who are relatively comfortable, who may feel our choices are proscribed by the cultures and systems in which we live. And yet, this is the calling of Jesus, a calling that is good news to the poor, but the rich often go away sad. Consider, however, the response of the tax collector Zacchaeus when he met Jesus (Luke 19): he gave away half his possessions and paid back four times what he had acquired unjustly (though legally) in the performance of his duties. He paid reparations to those whom he had taken advantage of through his position in society.

In our fast-paced world, where so often decisions are made with a goal of short-term profit, what does Christian faithfulness look like? Are we willing to hear Jesus' critique and focus our hearts rather than manipulating our profit margins?

Invitation:

Take inventory of where your money is invested. Do you have a bank, retirement, or other funds? Do they support fossil fuels or other companies causing harm to the planet? Consider reinvesting these funds in groups contributing to a sustainable and just future.

SEVENTH WEEK OF LENT: PALM SUNDAY

Becoming Rooted, Day 78,
"The Deer People"

As Jesus entered Jerusalem, the whole city was stirred to its
depths, demanding, "Who is this?" And the crowd kept answering,
"This is the prophet Jesus, from Nazareth in Galilee!"

—Matthew 21:10–11

In the most sacred stillness, I discerned the voice of all the
ages speaking words that reaffirmed the earlier decision I had
made so long ago, the one that changed my life direction.

—Randy Woodley, *Becoming Rooted*, 190–191

For your consideration: reading the Passion Story is like a dream experience. It's not about something that happened two thousand years ago; it's about something that's happening right now, like a mirror reflecting the very deepest parts of ourselves back at us through a glass darkly. As such, the encounter is by definition a psychedelic one: it's our own mind being made manifest, and every part of it—every single character—represents some part of us trying to find wholeness and completion inside the larger story. And today, that story starts with Palm Sunday.

Palm Sunday was the point of no return for Jesus: after three years of teaching, healing, and exorcising demons, he rides into Jerusalem like a conquering king out of the pages of ancient Scripture. Up until this time, Jesus has left some ambiguity as to his actual identity. Is he a prophet? A terrorist? The messiah? All these and more had been suggested, but Jesus was difficult to pin down. He spoke in poetry and in parable, and though he took on the garb of tradition, he re-arranged and re-tailored that tradition to match his unique revelation.

Up until Palm Sunday, anyone craving conflict with Rome would have been disappointed in Jesus, but poetry collides with political reality on the road to Jerusalem. Whatever deep mysteries Jesus hoped to reveal, he understood what his ultimate role was as his work reached its climax. Jesus decides to demonstrate this deeper purpose through direct conflict with the culture around him, even though he seems to know that this will be the death of him.

Two thousand years later, we are still living inside a passion story, a point of no return. Our worldview is in shambles, and we have to wrestle with the very real threat of societal collapse and maybe even human extinction. The Empire continues to crucify that which is most sacred to us, and in the face of this, each of us must decide what role we will play inside the larger story. We can no longer be part of the crowd that cheers for Jesus one day while calling for his execution the next. The Spirit is calling, and it calls us into conflict with the wider culture around us. Who is that still small voice asking you to become?

Invitation:

You may already know how to listen to the Spirit, but knowing how to do it and actually doing it are two different things. Given what time it is on the clock of the world, ask God who you are called to be and what you are called to do. Then listen.

SEVENTH WEEK OF LENT: MONDAY

Becoming Rooted, Day 79,
"Heart Desires"

Immediately upon coming out of the water, Jesus saw the heavens
opening and the Spirit descending on him like a dove. Then a voice
came from the heavens: "You are my Beloved, my Own. On you my
favor rests." Immediately the Spirit drove Jesus out into the wilderness,
and he remained there for forty days, and was tempted by Satan.
He was with the wild beasts, and the angels looked after him.

—Mark 1:10–13

As I listened to the birds, I began to hear a song in my own head.
"Unethlanahi yowegi" came to me, over and over again. Then more words
came, all in Cherokee. Before I knew it, I found myself singing this song...

—Randy Woodley, *Becoming Rooted*, 193

Some years back, I received a visitation from the Holy Spirit. The occasion was an ordination ceremony that I had been asked to preside over. Two friends were taking the plunge into ordained ministry, and it was part of my job to give them a "charge" (an inspirational mini-sermon) before releasing them into the wild as card-carrying clergy.

Yet something strange happened to me that morning as I began assembling and arranging the various robes, stoles, and Bibles that these two ministers-to-be were going to be presented with. I couldn't help but note a poignant irony regarding the stylized symbols we church-folk use to decorate our sacred objects. On that particular day, I saw doves, olive branches, and rushing wellsprings—metaphors perhaps, but metaphors taken directly from nature—and looking around the church, I saw half a dozen more of these symbols from nature.

But it dawned on me that as the liturgical and theological importance of these symbols had grown over the centuries, so too had their distance from the real world. My mind flashed back to the pillars and arches of Europe's medieval cathedrals, which were intended to evoke towering forest groves and canopies (trees that had to be cut down so that the very cathedrals evoking them could go up). From there, my mind drifted to the stained-glass birds, beasts, and vines that adorned my own church's rose window, which, in our case, wasn't even illuminated by sunlight but rather by a thousand-watt electronic lightbox.

As the Spirit would have it, the ordination charge I ended up delivering that Sunday wasn't exactly the same one I had prepared. As I formally sent my two friends off into their new lives of ministry, I looked at their flowing vestments and eager countenances and felt newly compelled to urge them: Don't trust pictures of doves. Trust real doves. Don't trust stained-glass windows whose frames have been hammered into the shape of a rose or that depict elegantly creeping vines or gentle lambs. Trust real roses, and real vines, and real lambs—things that actually breathe and eat and drink and live and die. Whatever you do, don't trust in your lofty ideas about this world or in your abstracted liturgical metaphors about what it means to be living in it. Trust only—and always—in the real thing.

Invitation:

What if you allowed for the possibility that creation—not the Bible—is God's primary text? If that is true, here is a simple practice: go outside and see what it's telling you.

SEVENTH WEEK OF LENT: TUESDAY

Becoming Rooted, Day 81,
"The Directions"

Jesus insisted that the disciples get into the boat and precede him
to the other side. Having sent the crowds away, he went up on the
mountain by himself to pray, remaining there alone as night fell.

—Matthew 14:22–23

[I]n Sunday school, when I was first taught to pray, I was told to
fold my hands, bow my head, and close my eyes. Later...I learned
to pray with my eyes open and by facing the seven directions:
east, south, west, north, sky, Earth, and then, for myself.

—Randy Woodley, *Becoming Rooted*, 199

On a recent camping trip to Glacier National Park, I had two profound experiences. The first one almost everyone gets when they go out into the wilderness: an overwhelming sense of peace and calm, as if all the anxiety and stress is being sucked out of your body. Why does this happen so consistently when we walk out of our cities? Why does it take us getting out to realize we're going mad?

But the other thing that no one can miss in Glacier National Park is the fact that the park is melting. Quickly. This is a place where family photos taken one year, when compared to photos taken at the same place the following year, shockingly reveal just how fast our ancient glaciers are shrinking. This is a place where you can swim in hidden lakes formed from snow that has not been in liquid form for ten thousand years, and the hiking paths are being perpetually re-routed around new streams and rivers surging off the mountains. It's a dramatic object lesson, to say the least, but even there—in this elaborate diorama of global warming—you can overhear Christian youth group leaders telling their students to disregard what the Park Rangers are saying to visitors. All this has nothing to do with us, they say; all this is part of God's plan.

So today, I want us to consider—for a lot of reasons—the possibility that our Christian gospel needs to become a green gospel. The good news quickly becomes bad news if it isn't rooted in the real world. And here's a very simple idea to help guide us into these waters: theology, if it is to have any real-world meaning to us, must now be re-interpreted as ecology, in the fullest sense of that word. Here ecology means acknowledging the true interdependence of all people, institutions, and the natural world. It is the recognition, as Christ teaches us, that we are all part of a larger body and that what happens to one part of creation directly impacts the rest of creation. Because of this, as people of faith, we are called not only to be our brothers' keepers and our sisters' keepers, we are called to be creation's keepers as well. Theology—if it is to have any kind of integrity as a comforter and a guide—must equal ecology.

Invitation:

How would your own faith tradition and practice look if theology = ecology? How would that change your experience of prayer and your reading of sacred Scripture? If you're uncertain, take your Bible outside, read it, and see what happens.

SEVENTH WEEK OF LENT: WEDNESDAY

Becoming Rooted, Day 86,
"Invasives"

The work I do in my Abba's name gives witness in my favor,
but you don't believe because you're not my sheep. My sheep
hear my voice. I know them, and they follow me.

—John 10:25b–27

Although the invasive species are not originally from this land, we try
to understand their purpose, and we watch how they interact with the
native plants.…[If] the species learns to interact well with…the rest of
the community of creation, we allow more of the population to flourish.

—Randy Woodley, *Becoming Rooted*, 210

I have a picture at home that tells a whole story about Christianity's history on this continent. The picture is of my own great-great-grandfather, Rev. G.W. Alcorn, a circuit preacher to the so-called "Indian Nation" of Oklahoma. No one living today can remember Rev. Alcorn, but his story is told by the two heirlooms he has handed down: a Bible and a gun.

It's a horror story. The Bible and the gun became domesticating agents for an expanding United States, and in so doing, the gospel of Jesus was again co-opted to serve the same kind of Empire it was born to resist. For my whole life, my family has been deeply ashamed of this story. But as a kind of invasive species here in North America, if we are to ever become rooted, we must first acknowledge the legacy of violence we brought with us, make amends for it, and learn how to live in right relationship with all our neighbors.

In truth, something about our worldview made it impossible for us to really *see* the cultures that lived here before us, and tremendous harm was done in that blindness. Our actions not only decimated the First Peoples of this land, but today the blindness of this worldview threatens all life because we can't really see ourselves, either. The worldwide web of our military/consumer culture has become so abstracted from place, so removed from our true dependence on the land that our entire civilization is now in a state of emergency.

Environmentalist Ray Dasmann has some useful terms to help distinguish between the worldviews of Indigenous cultures, which he calls "ecosystem-based cultures," and city-state cultures, which he calls "biosphere cultures." The chief difference is between a society whose life and wisdom are all centered around a specific natural region and watershed, and those other cultures (like ours) who discovered that rather than adapting to the changing environmental demands of one's own region, it might be easier to just spill over into another region, another watershed, another people's territory, and steal away its resources, natural or human.

So perhaps it's no accident that the Bible has so often been paired with the gun. But what does it look like to disarm our sacred Scriptures? And what new heirlooms can we be handing down along with them to the next generation?

Invitation:

How did your family come to North America? When and where did they come? What were the resources they used, and who were the people originally on the land they settled in? We can't look forward without first looking back.

SEVENTH WEEK OF LENT: MAUNDY THURSDAY

Becoming Rooted, Day 84,
"Religion and Spirituality"

My little children, I won't be with you much longer. You'll look for me, but what I said to the Temple authorities, I say to you: where I am going, you cannot come. I give you a new commandment: Love one another. And you're to love one another the way I have loved you. This is how all will know that you're my disciples: that you truly love one another.

—John 13:33–35

As for me, I choose the camp of uncertainty. I leave Great Mystery to be explored and humbly understood and known as best I can.

—Randy Woodley, *Becoming Rooted*, 206

As the story goes, Jesus knew this was their final night together. Jesus knew he was going to die, that the heavy hand of the Empire was about to come down on all of them, and that his disciples were waiting for the same kind of deliverance that came for their ancestors under Pharaoh. I imagine that any of the standard Biblical tricks would have done it. But in this moment, Jesus doesn't summon a plague, nor does he wait to see if God will send locusts. Instead, he offers a very different kind of deliverance in his own unique Exodus story. In this version, Jesus is not content to defer to some all-powerful God up in the clouds at this moment, nor does he wait for a battalion of angels to rescue him. Rather he says that in this story, the sacred "I am that which I am" is the God within me, and the God within you, and that God's deliverance can only be found in this: in the love that we have for one another.

This, I believe, is the climax of the Passion Story. And recognizing ourselves in this story, we acknowledge that, thousands of years later, all our holy lands are still contested by strife and violence and that the oppressors and oppressed have switched roles so many times we can't even tell which ones we are anymore. We can only know with certainty that we as a people have not found deliverance yet. By shifting our focus back to Maundy Thursday, we are forced to accept where we really are in the story: in the midst of it, unsure, unknowing, three days before the event we hope for, but one day before the event we dread.

But when we acknowledge and accept our vulnerability and our helplessness, Jesus' "new commandment" to his friends reveals itself as a different kind of salvation. Not as an intellectual "answer" or any other kind of party-line that can be shared with others in little pamphlets. But salvation as a living, breathing mystery that can only be revealed between us, among us, and within us. Salvation as an experience you can't get by being loved by some far-away God up in the sky, or by being right, but only by learning to love others—and to be loved—right here on the ground.

Invitation:

Break bread with people you love and trust, recognizing that when you do, the meal becomes a holy sacrament and that this is a gift of love and deliverance from the Great Mystery.

SEVENTH WEEK OF LENT: GOOD FRIDAY

Becoming Rooted, Day 82,
"Life, Death, and Now"

[Pilate] went back into the Praetorium and asked Jesus, "Where do you come from?" Jesus didn't answer. Then Pilate said to Jesus, "You refuse to speak? Bear in mind that I have the power to release you—and to crucify you." "You would have no authority over me," Jesus replied, "unless it had been given to you by God. Therefore the person who handed me over to you has the greater sin."

—John 19:9–11

Death is simply another part of living. Because death is truly sad, we don't like to think about it. But death is our reality and life continues after that. Perhaps winter is meant to remind us that life is bigger than ourselves.

—Randy Woodley, *Becoming Rooted*, 202

Something happens to us when we look death in the eye. And it's terrible, and it's messy, and it can be the very last thing in the world any of us wants to do. But there is no getting away from it, and when it comes for each of us—in one way or another—we have to choose whether we're going to keep running from it or whether we're going to turn around and let it transform us.

Today we reflect on one of the big ideas of gospel spirituality, maybe the central truth around which all the other spiritual truths constellate themselves. In order to save your life, first, you must lose it. In order to truly experience life, first, you must face death. Jesus calls this "picking up your cross," but there are, of course, countless other ways to talk about it.

For the Buddhists, ignoring the reality of death is part of a spiritual sickness called "*samsara*," which they believe infects our species with a kind of amnesia. In this view, humans can only remember their true nature when they embrace their own mortality (or "impermanence") because this unveils the ebb and flow of a larger ocean of consciousness beyond our notions of "birth" and "death." In traditional Christian theology, death is described as the side-effect of an ancient curse called "sin." But in this way of thinking, death is more about a broken relationship, a failure to acknowledge that we don't really exist independently as the little separate egos we've made up for ourselves. For Christians, we are mended only when we "die unto ourselves" and accept our larger life in God.

Both of these descriptions are fine as far as I'm concerned. But of course, it's easier to talk about facing death than to actually do it. Fear of death becomes a kind of nameless horror in the back of our brains, something that plagues our whole lives with fear, depression, anxiety, or any of the things that we run from but which eventually get us in the end. Thus our unwillingness to face death becomes another kind of death. When we fail to recognize how much of our lives are spent up in the illusory pursuit of self-preservation and self-promotion, we fail to recognize how much these fears and denials cost our experience of living.

Invitation:

Today let us remember that something miraculous happens to us when we look death in the eye. The opportunities to do this will find you, but today try not to avoid them.

SEVENTH WEEK OF LENT: HOLY SATURDAY

Becoming Rooted, Day 90,
"Original Instructions"

This much have I said to you while still with you; but the Paraclete,
the Holy Spirit whom Abba God will send in my name, will instruct
you in everything and she will remind you of all that I told you.

—John 14:25–26

I think, whether by divine decree or as human experience
evolved—or maybe both—all indigenous people, everywhere,
came to understand something from their interactions with
the Earth: that living in harmony is the best way to live and,…
the only way to live that will sustain us into a hopeful future.

—Randy Woodley, *Becoming Rooted*, 219

How's this for a crucifixion story? In the summer of 1991, twenty-five miles off the Northwest Coast of Washington State, a Chinese freighter collided with the Japanese fishing vessel Tenyo Maru. When this happened, the Tenyo Maru quickly sank, but as it did, it began releasing hundreds of thousands of gallons of fuel directly into the ocean, and most of this ended up coating the shores of Washington State and parts of Oregon.

I was a teenager at the time, but I remember this incident very well. I remember seeing the spill, seeing how much of the coastal wildlife it was killing, and some part of me just seized up. A deep despair washed over me, a feeling of inevitability and hopelessness, and for much of my life, the image of that oil spill worked inside me as a kind of archetypal placeholder for all the human-made horrors I felt completely powerless at stopping.

But how's this for a resurrection story? Did you know that there is something called an Oyster Mushroom, which grows throughout North America, and which has the unique, naturally occurring ability to clean up oil spills by leaching them up as food? And did you also know that these same mushrooms, once grown by eating up all the oil, are still completely edible for humans to eat? It's amazing but true. More funding is needed to really develop it practically, but the basic science works. There are mushrooms that can naturally break down, clean up, and detoxify oil, all the while producing a healthy food source.

So consider this a free gift from the Holy Spirit. The thought of these little oil-eating mushrooms resonated with me so deeply that I saw in a vision the whole beach back in Washington State entirely covered with them. And this vision shifted something deep inside me; some old wound healed over. For the first time in I don't know how long, I knew that God was going to deliver us. The road might be rocky, but I became filled with certainty and deep relief that the planet is still producing the miracles it needs to survive, and so can we.

EASTER SUNDAY

Becoming Rooted, Day 98,
"The Value of Now"

No sooner had [Mary of Magdala] said this than she turned around and caught sight of Jesus standing there, but she didn't know it was Jesus. He asked her, "Why are you weeping? For whom are you looking?" She supposed it was the gardener so she said, "Please, if you're the one who carried Jesus away, tell me where you've laid the body and I will take it away."

—John 20:14–15

That this idea of a new body is present in so many religions surprises me. Given the last three thousand years and the influence of Platonic dualism on Western thinking, I am somewhat shocked to know the human thread of persistence still conceives us as a whole being.

—Randy Woodley, *Becoming Rooted*, 237

Our gospel tradition literally claims that Jesus not only came back from the dead three days after he died but that when he did come back, he could apparently look like different things to different people. In some versions, Mary Magdalene mistakes him for a gardener or an Angel outside the tomb. Later, two of his students mistake him for a "stranger on the road" for the better part of a day. The text falls short of literally claiming that Jesus came back as a shape-shifter. But it's as if, on some level, Jesus dies and then comes back as everybody so that everybody is now the Christ, everybody is now the savior, and everybody we meet—including ourselves—is God's infinite care incarnated in human form. And maybe that isn't so radical given that Jesus directly suggests that this is the case in Matthew 25 when he says, "Whatever you do to the least of these you are doing to me."

Through this possibility, the gospel invites us directly into the living heart of the world through every act of kind accompaniment. The story asks us to consider the possibility that compassion and interconnectedness are the deepest realities of our universe, and that in comparison, things like time, space, history, and identity are all convenient cover stories, whose only true value is to express our deeper communion. The Bible asks us to consider not only that God is real, but that God is here, taking the form of all of us and the whole community of creation; and that God is discovered only when we learn how to break bread and make peace with all of God's parts in equal measure. And I'm not asking you to take my word on any of this, or the Bible's, but I do invite all you to find out for yourself, first-hand, whether or not this is true. Because everything changes if it is.

Invitation:

Try on the idea that everyone you meet today is, in fact, the Christ—and not just part of them, but all of them, their whole being. And consider: why has Jesus decided to come back in this way? What lessons are being passed on? What is the Spirit trying to teach you about connecting heaven and Earth?

SCRIPTURE INDEX

CPSIA information can be obtained
at www.ICGtesting.com
Printed in the USA
BVHW070853160122
625954BV00005B/22

9 781594 980831